Olives to Lychees
Everyday Mediter-asian Spa Cuisine
Volume 2

THE ART OF FEELING WELL:
HOW TO GET THINGS MOVING WHEN YOU FEEL *S.T.U.C.K.*
(STRESSED, TIRED, UNWELL OR UPSET, CRANKY, KNOCKED DOWN)
FOR OPTIMAL NOURISHMENT, NURTURANCE AND WELLNESS
OF MIND, BODY AND SPIRIT

MARIE-CLAIRE BOURGEOIS

Balboa Press books may be ordered through booksellers or by contacting:

Balboa Press
A Division of Hay House
1663 Liberty Drive
Bloomington, IN 47403
www.balboapress.com
1 (877) 407-4847

ISBN: 978-1-5043-4169-1 (sc)
ISBN: 978-1-5043-4173-8 (e)

Library of Congress Control Number: 2015920855

Print information available on the last page.

Balboa Press rev. date: 3/8/2016

BALBOA
PRESS
A DIVISION OF HAY HOUSE

Table of Contents

Dedications

To all those who need to carve time out in their stressful lives for self-care,
may this book on the Art of Feeling Well
be the encouragement they need to create and maintain a regular home spa ritual
for the nourishment of the mind, the body and the spirit.

To all those who are struggling with health and weight issues
despite their best effort to regain and maintain optimal wellness levels,
may this book offer a fresh mindset, answers and solutions.

To all those who don't know how to cook or don't cook much,
may this book offer the inspiration and the motivation
to develop this important life skill
and have fun preparing delicious and nourishing meals.

To all the health-conscious foodies who love to cook and eat fresh food,
may this book be a resource
for inspired creativity, optimal wellness,
and the Art and the Pleasure of eating well.

To Philip, my Sweet Love,
The best friend and most caring life partner I could ever wish for.
Thank you for always being so supportive in all my projects.
Feeling your loving presence next to me and hearing your steady encouragements
enable me to climb any mountain with confidence and perseverance.
I am at my best when I am with you.
You are my gentle giant.
Love you always.

M~C

Foreword

As *The New York Times Best-Selling Author* of many financial books over thirty years, I have made a career and a fortune teaching people how to be financially wealthy. I also teach my students that taking care of themselves is crucial to their financial success. As part of a healthy lifestyle, we all need to develop and practice a daily "rich-ual" consisting of physical exercises, nutritious meals, meditation, prayers, and positive affirmations to ensure that one's energy is grounded, positive, and receptive to Divine guidance.

As I've often said, *Your Health is Your Wealth*. Anyone who has experienced illness would attest that without good health, it is more challenging to achieve your goals, and fulfill your life purpose. Investing in yourself and in your health is always encouraged as it ensures a brighter future. Along with a regular exercise program that suits you, one of the best health investments you can make is through proper nourishment and eating habits.

I met Marie-Claire at two of my "Fortune In You" workshops where she passionately introduced me to the concept of this book. She is absolutely amazing! Having the opportunity to try many different cuisines from around the world during my speaking and coaching engagements, I feel that this book is a gift to all of you health-conscious foodies who love to cook and eat great food to enjoy steady health.

In this book, Marie-Claire provides the reasons why we all need to nourish ourselves, as our ancestors did, with the basic essentials: fresh produce, organically grown meats, oils, nuts and seeds. She guides you on how to take better care of yourself by getting back to basics, and developing "the Art of Feeling Well" with a regular spa care ritual based on nine health-building blocks. She believes that a healthy lifestyle is the stepping stone to becoming more of what we are meant to be. Her creative ways of blending the amazing flavours of the Mediterranean and Asian regions into simple healing dishes and care products make this spa book unique, timely and, best of all, healthful.

This book will inspire you to create your own daily gourmet spa food and spa care products to regain *and* maintain wellness. You will feel well nourished and pampered (and who doesn't like to feel pampered?), just like at the spa, but for a fraction of the cost and in the comfort of your home. I know it will transform your health and, ultimately, your life.

Robert G. Allen
#1 Best-selling author, speaker, mentor
The Fortune In You
Author of *Cash in a Flash*
www.RobertAllen.com
San Diego, 2014

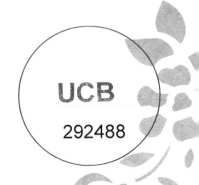

v

Part 1
A- Creating a Spa Experience at Home

**for a brief moment, a few hours, a day, or a weekend
to reduce and manage stress,
and to nourish the mind, the body and the spirit**

Imagine being in a peaceful environment that invites you to focus on your authentic self, your needs and your wishes… away from stressful distractions and concerns…

Imagine a place where you can "retreat" and take time out to enjoy a calming mini-vacation where your body and mind gradually shift from feeling "heavy and cluttered" to "light and clear"…

Imagine this blissful time out allowing you to nurture, nourish and replenish the whole YOU -- mind, body and spirit -- so you can re-enter your world of regular activities with renewed perspective and energy…

Would that feel like heaven? But, does that sound impossible?

Let's breathe for a moment…

I invite you to make yourself comfortable where you are sitting to read this book, and take a few deep belly breaths… As you relax, ask yourself which part of you needs some loving care and nourishment at this time.

Is it the Stressed one? The Tired one? The Upset one?

Is it the Unwell one? The Cranky one? Or is it the Knocked down one?

I want you to know that all are welcome at this time in this space.

It is not as impossible as it sounds to experience heaven on earth. In fact, I have a wellness plan, a "Nourishment Therapy", to make it possible for you; a plan that goes beyond the terry-cloth robe, the fuzzy slippers and the cucumber slices over the eyes. If followed, this plan goes beyond the pampering routines as it can change the way you manage your stress, how you care for yourself, and how you breathe and relax. It can change the way you eat, and the quality of your life. The transformational wellness-enhancing tools that I offer in my plan can help you experience heaven on earth in your home *whenever you want*. Shifting from caring for everyone else to caring for yourself, even for just a half hour a day, to do the things you truly enjoy and find relaxing can be rejuvenating and "health-changing". I am offering you a life-style adjustment to regain and maintain balance and wellness.

If You Have Stress in Your Life, You Need to Take Time Out

I am sure that, as it is the case for most people, your life is extremely busy with more and more work, activities, expectations and responsibilities being crammed into your already full schedule. I believe that more than ever we need to regularly slow down, stop and take time out to reconnect with ourselves, and figure out what we need to feel better and, ultimately, feel our best. Is it a day off away from children or aging parents so you can sleep or read a book peacefully? Is it a massage? A vacation? A long hot bath? What else? I bet it has something to do with the 5 Rs: Rest and Relaxation, Repair, Rejuvenation, and Re-creation.

The key to feeling better is the willingness to give ourselves what we need. In my holistic health practice, I often have clients, mostly females, who complain of what I summarize as the "*S.T.U.C.K.* symptoms" – *Stressed, Tired, Unwell or Upset, Cranky, Knocked down.* They are seeking answers, solutions and guidance. However, a big challenge they face is that they find receiving loving care and attention quite challenging. As care givers raising children and nurturing aging parents, they have been in a "giving mode" for so long that they don't know how to receive or what receiving without guilt feels like. Some of them have been under so much stress for so long that they don't know they are stressed out and running on empty. Consequently, they feel unhappy, depleted, used, frustrated, and often resentful. Life is about giving and receiving; we can't always be the giver, or the receiver of life's abundance. We have to find the balance between the two that works for us. Women, mothers in particular, after so many years of giving of themselves, of their time and their loving energy to others, often express the need to focus on replenishing themselves, receiving loving attention and pleasure, and HAVING FUN. Many want the opportunity to focus on manifesting their own dreams and wishes. Going to a spa or creating one at home is the perfect opportunity to fulfill this need for well-deserved nurturance – loving and affectionate care and attention. In fact, I am making this suggestion to anyone who is busy looking after the needs of others, has a lot of responsibilities, and little or no time for themselves.

The spa suggestions that you will find in this book are focusing on the *therapeutic* aspects of restoring and healing the mind, the body and the spirit rather than on the esthetics. I believe that when you feel great on the inside – when you are increasingly more aware of your inner beauty, your essence, and your meaningful life purpose -- it is reflected on the outside: a spiritual radiance and steady energy that make people curious to know what you are doing, and eager to experience the same results.

For our long-term wellness, we need to learn how to give to ourselves and receive from others. HOW?

- *By starting to take time for ourselves.* Not too long ago, I was handed a fortune cookie that reads, *"You will be happiest if you please yourself first."* It may sounds selfish but it is quite the opposite. Just as passengers are instructed at the beginning of a flight, in the event of an unforeseen situation, to put their own oxygen mask on themselves first so they can assist others, it is when we look after ourselves on a regular basis that we are better able to serve others, without resentment or feel like a martyr. This feeling of resentment permeates everything we do and our relationships, leaving no one happy. When we generously give to ourselves and we regularly take time to replenish our energy reservoir, we become happier. We, then, have plenty to give others, without the fear of running on empty. We can all find a minimum of 10-15 minutes each day for personal time out to rest, reflect, pamper, recharge and rejuvenate; even if it is in the shower or on the toilet! (If you have time to go on Facebook or watch evening drama shows on television, you have time to look after yourself!) And for super busy or stressed individuals, they need to double the "rest-and-recharge" time! In my opinion, this 15-minute "rest-and-recharge" time needs to be enjoyed mindfully without distractions like books, newspaper, TV, screens (Internet, phone, tablet), drink, food, nicotine, recreational or medicinal drugs. This precious quiet time could be spent sitting or lying down with eyes closed, doing several deep belly breaths to still the mind and the body.
- *By asking for what we need and want*: time out, assistance with household chores, loving attention, emotional support, a raise, babysitting services, etc.
- *By graciously and gratefully accepting what others willingly offer.*

Look at this time out as an investment in your self-love and self-care, and a treat or reward after your hard day's work, shifting from being of service to others in the daytime to pampering the princess (or the prince!) in you in the evening. Or whenever you can let her/him out.

Create a Spa-care Fund to Invest in You and in Your Wellness

Speaking of investment, women seem to be willing to generously invest in a variety of things and activities: mortgage, home renovation, a car, car maintenance, after-school programs for the children, gifts for others, charity donations, etc. However, when the time comes to spend some money on themselves, most of them feel quite uncomfortable, guilty and even selfish. Perhaps creating a *Spa-care Fund* would alleviate this problem as the money set aside could cover the cost of health-enhancing purchases and experiences that nourish the physical, emotional and spiritual being, such as massages and other therapeutic sessions, haircuts, cosmetics, organic foods, supplements, essential oils, exercise classes, exercise equipment, a visit to the spa, a weekend retreat, etc. Decide what you want and how much of a reserve you need. As much as you can, set some money aside for nurturing yourself on a regular basis. Perhaps you can let go of a habit you have been meaning to get rid of or an unnecessary expense, and transfer the savings to your Spa-care Fund. Another way to increase the Spa-care Fund is to add a portion of any unexpected windfalls you may receive such as monetary gifts, refunds, bonuses, extra income, etc. And when family members and friends ask you what you would like for your birthday, Christmas or Mother's Day, tell them what you would *really* like: a special book, a gift certificate to your favorite store, cash to go towards a spa day, babysitting services for an afternoon or an evening out. Since they are willing to spend money to make you happy, give them the chance to do so and accept graciously their expression of love for you. So, next time that you feel Stressed, Tired, Unwell, Upset, Cranky, or Knocked down, you will have the funds reserved for well-deserved nurturance and restoring moments.

It is from a state of relaxation, in a safe and sacred space away from the daily stresses and worries,
that the body's energy is free to flow, and healing and restoration take place.

Why Create Your Own Spa Experience at Home

By creating your own spa experience at home, there is no need to travel far; you can take time for yourself as often as possible, even if it is just for a few hours, and at minimal cost. Block off some time in your schedule, unplug the phone and disconnect from the outside world. If you have children, make arrangements with family members or close neighbours to look after them. You can arrange babysitting exchanges with other parents to look after your children while you enjoy a free evening or weekend of R & R. When those parents need an evening or a weekend off, you make arrangements to return the favour.

This second volume of nourishment for wellness is designed to inspire you to take great care of yourself so you feel healthier, more vibrant and happier; in other words, the best possible version of yourself -- as you are meant to be. In my practice, I invite clients to schedule regular "appointments" with themselves and create their own daily self-care ritual. As caregivers, it is so easy for you to fall in the habit of scheduling your lives around everyone else's and putting yourself last. In order to continue being of service to others, you must make time for yourself, and keep those appointments. It is also important to model this stress management and self-care practice for the children and teenagers so they learn how to prevent getting over-stressed, burned-out, and becoming ill. It doesn't matter how sophisticated the technology becomes; we still need and will always need basic stress management skills. Creating regular pauses in our fast-paced lives ensures that we continue the journey without breaking down.

There is nothing wrong in falling,
as long as you keep rising every time you fall.

Developing and maintaining a stress management self-care routine is essential to effectively deal with life's challenges instead of turning to drugs and alcohol, unhealthy foods, and destructive behaviours to dull and numb painful feelings. It can empower and ground you; it can also help you bring your stress under control while you find balance and a life purpose in the middle of chaos. Taking some time out to reflect and recharge can be used to re-evaluate your path in life so far and decide if a change in direction is needed. Taking time out to reflect and recharge helps you develop higher self-awareness, focus and mindfulness that will enhance your wellness while enriching every aspect of your daily experience.

What Does "a Balanced Life" Mean to You?

How would you describe your life at the moment? How close is this description to the picture of the dream life that you have envisioned? What would you like to change so your reality is closer to your dream life? There are as many definitions or descriptions of "a balanced life" as there are individuals. The descriptions vary from spending as much time at work as possible, to devoting all available time with family members, to needing to escape to be alone once in a while with nothing to do. (My definition is a regular escape in nature with nothing to do!) Some people even believe that there is no such thing as *balance* or *a balanced life!*

In my opinion, balance fluctuates with the quantity and the quality of time and energy that we use. Feeling overwhelmed by the weight of too many responsibilities, expectations, and the pressure to perform at work is unfortunately very common in our modern fast-paced society. Shouldering all this heavy pressure (with or without complaints) does not contribute to the quality of our lives and does not warrant us a medal or an epitaph on our tombstone. We need to believe that we have the power to control our lives and make choices, including the choice to change our attitude regarding a stressful situation so it does not wear us down.

Feelings of unhappiness, frustration, exhaustion, and resentment indicate that something is not right in the way our life is going. This *imbalance* most likely stems from the gap between what we perceive our current life to be and what we truly need or want. In our over-consuming society, we are strongly encouraged to invest a lot of money, energy and time on aspiring to *have* more – more money, more relationships, bigger house, more material things, bigger promotions, etc. – to a point that we shush and squash the inner wise part of ourselves that tells us what we need to do to take care of *ourselves,* to be well and truly happy. When we shush and push aside the inner wise part of ourselves, we tend to focus on what we don't have yet. I believe that, in order to acknowledge and nourish that inner part, we need to regularly *be* still, go back to basics, "think inside the box" and reflect on the following 10 questions:

- Where am I in my life journey?
- Am I happy?

- What do I really want and need?
- What are my main priorities right now?
- Am I living my life the way I have imagined it? What are my dreams?
- When will I have enough?
- What matters most in my life right now?
- What do I value?
- Is what I am chasing really important, and will it matter in three to five years (give a specific date i.e., on February 15, whatever year) from now?
- What may I regret later in my life?

My life is not perfect, but I view it as very good! To feel balanced, *I need time out*, at least one hour a day to do what *I* want! Otherwise, I get cranky.

To feel balanced, my life must also include, among many things, sufficient time and opportunities for:

- holistic wellness and nourishment (body care; time to daydream, to read, to cook, to be in nature, etc.);
- relationship with myself, Philip, family, friends and clients;
- personal growth, and realizing my potential and dreams.

My life feels fairly harmonious when I am living according to what I value most, and when I have adjusted my attitude to one of gratitude. When life throws me an unexpectedly huge challenge, to get through it and maintain a sense of balance while riding the storm, I use every skill I have and ask for help when I have exhausted my resources. Once the storm has passed – they all do, eventually – I thank the Divine for the learning and the growth experience, and celebrate. For Philip and I, it is important to live our lives to the beat of our own drums and tune out the noise of external influence and pressure. By determining what our values and dreams are, setting clear priorities, and saying "No" when we need to, we are able to enjoy a life that is less stressed and more meaningful. We feel incredibly blessed and grateful to the Divine for each other and our lives. We know that love and gratitude are powerful magnets for life's abundance.

When the Universe Has New Plans for You

At the time that I am writing these lines, Philip and I have been experiencing unexpected health challenges affecting our four parents. It has been a relentless test of strength, stamina, patience and compassion. We know it is the beginning of a long journey to support and care for our parents in the last chapters of their lives. With the help of Philip's siblings and partners, we can get through the tough times with his parents. On my side, my father and I are allowing family, friends and neighbours to support and carry us when needed. We accept graciously and gratefully their help in whatever form it comes. We have helped so many people up to this day; it is our turn to need loving assistance.

Focus on the song in your heart and tune out the surrounding noise.

Being Perfectly Imperfect!

I admit that, sometimes in periods of heavy stress, I need reminders to focus on the song in my heart and to elevate my spirits! I remind myself that I am perfectly imperfect and it is normal to get tired and frustrated, to feel disorganized and unproductive, to cry and want to run away. Even though I work in the wellness and stress management field and feel it is important to model a good example, I have to shush that nasty "self-flagellating" voice inside my head and remind myself to stop, be still, breathe, notice what is going on inside my body, acknowledge my state of mind, and determine how I can rise above the not-so-positive feelings to lift my spirit. Like everyone else, I often feel tested, stressed and overwhelmed, and sometimes sick, by life events. Accepting that I am human reduces the stress to have "it" all together, all the time. What I learn from managing the stressful life events is what I share with others who are experiencing similar situations.

For many years, I was thinking that I could resume my "regular movement therapy", my self-care ritual and my meditation only *after* completing this big project or *after* this course … or when I had free time. Was I ever fooling myself! I realized that my day-to-day living is a proof that there will always be lots of things to get through on my schedule, that there never is a *perfect time* to take care of myself, exercise and meditate. It is up to me to schedule the movement therapy and self-care ritual times like bookends: first thing in the morning before starting the day's activities and before bedtime to reflect on the day and settle the nervous system in preparation for a good night of sleep. Realizing that I, a busy woman like you, will never have an ideal schedule forces me to become more committed and disciplined to create and maintain a self-care routine that helps me get back in balance.

In order to be happy, fit, well put together and able to face the daily challenges, I needed to see this self-care routine as a discipline, just like I would if I wanted to become an artist or a musician. Practice… is what trains us to improve our skills whether it is in cooking, playing a sport or a musical instrument, or enhancing our wellness with meditation and self-care. Enhancing my wellness is a lot easier than mastering the piano or playing tennis. Walking, gardening and cooking are my regular activities that allow me to still my mind, be present, mindful and connected to my being. To thrive, we have to include the "feel good" activities in our daily schedule and honour them as best as possible, just as we honour the other commitments, so we stay out of the doctor's office and the emergency room.

Developing and maintaining a nourishing self-care routine is a great strategy to reduce stress and find peace and balance in your daily life. To bring more peace and balance in your life and prevent overbooking yourself, I suggest that, as much as possible, for every item that you add to your schedule or workload, you remove something. Otherwise, as you know, the schedule becomes fuller with still only 24 hours in a day, and a limited amount of energy to accomplish everything. Trying to do it all and have it all is exhausting and stressful; it prevents you from enjoying life, what you currently have, and the people you care about. Pace yourself to the sound of your own drum beat!

In Volume 1, I focused on the Art and the Pleasure of Eating Well and discussed:

1. WHY it is important, *more than ever*,

   - to learn how to cook if your skills are "under-developed";
   - to plan to cook more often, to create basic foods from scratch;
   - to know what to eat, how to eat by adopting a "fresher" approach towards food, nutrition and nourishment with the Paleo Nourishment and Lifestyle Plan to resolve health issues; and

2. HOW you can make your Healthy Mediter-asian Spa Cuisine a part of your lifestyle to experience the Art and the Pleasure of Eating Well.

In this Volume, I am focusing on the Art of Feeling Well to deal with life's stressful challenges. You will learn:

1. WHY creating a spa experience at home is important for your relaxation, stress management and wellness;
2. HOW to nourish and rejuvenate mind, body and spirit by balancing your elements;
3. HOW to develop your own Spa Care Ritual to get things moving when you feel *S.T.U.C.K. – Stressed, Tired, Unwell or Upset, Cranky, Knocked Down* -- with the 5 Rs: Relax, Release stress, Recharge/Restore, Rejuvenate, and Re-create using a few simple techniques and recipes to create your own Mediterranean and Asian-inspired body care products with natural ingredients;
4. HOW easy it is to create your own Spa Cuisine to keep you hydrated and well-nourished;
5. HOW your Spa Cuisine can support your healthy lifestyle and the Art of Feeling Well during your pampering ritual and every day after.

My mission

- To share wellness and nourishment tips as well as deliciously easy recipes to support a healthy and meaningful lifestyle.
- To encourage you to take time out to relax, de-stress and pamper yourself on a regular basis so you feel rejuvenated, happier and more vibrant. Allow Mother Nature to nourish YOU -- mind, body and spirit!

The ability to heal and the power of rejuvenation that we all possess
are triggered when the body is in a state of relaxation and deep rest.

B- Nourishing and Rejuvenating Mind, Body and Spirit by Balancing the Elements

If you are currently experiencing health and wellness challenges, it means that something in your life or lifestyle needs to be adjusted, and that you are getting ready for a shift. I believe that is why this book resonated with you when you picked it up.

We are not designed to sustain constant stress without regular and significant periods of relaxation, restoration and re-creation. Even machines need regular rest periods and tune-ups to maximize their performance and minimize wear and tear. Life is so much harder when we try to share our unique talents and gifts with the world and we become challenged with pain, heavy stress, exhaustion, upset, and discomfort in our bodies.

Signs of Overstress - Are you experiencing any of these signs?

Modern lifestyle can contribute to the buildup of chronic overstress that produces numerous physical, mental, emotional and spiritual disturbances and discomfort in the body, mind and spirit. The overstress signs act as warning signals indicating that something requires your attention. If ignored, the signals become stronger, "louder" and harder to disregard. Here are a few:

- muscle tension in the neck and shoulders causing pain and stiffness;
- muscle tension in the scalp and jaw resulting in headaches, migraines;
- teeth grinding at night, nail biting, fidgeting and foot tapping;
- faster heart beats, shallow breathing, sweating;
- digestive problems resulting in indigestion, heartburn, irritable bowel syndrome (IBS), bowel disturbances;
- a feeling of constant pressure to keep going;
- tiredness, low energy, anxiety, irritability, depression, constant worrying, racing mind that can't become still;
- insomnia, disturbed sleep patterns;
- panic attacks;
- disturbed appetite;
- increased alcohol or drug intake that may lead to substance dependence;
- skin irruptions;
- inexplicable pain and discomfort, etc.

If you are experiencing some of these signs of stress, I bet you have been trying several methods, including medications, to alleviate these symptoms without any long-lasting results. Since you are reading this book, I guess that you would like to find natural solutions to regain the vitality, the comfort and the ease in your body that you once had, as well as a general feeling of wellness. Am I right? Keep reading to learn how to create **health-building blocks** that promote the 5 Rs: Relaxation, Release of stress, Restoration, Rejuvenation, and Re-creation of the body, mind and spirit. But first, I need to introduce you to the elements. And they are…

Earth, Water, Fire, Air … and Ether

I am sure you have heard of the first four elements but not so much about the last one. According to Ayurveda, a traditional healing system of India, all five elements are constantly present in our bodies, in nature, and in every living being. They exist in various amounts and qualities, are interdependent of one another, and, like the weather, are constantly in movement and changing.

When one or more elements are in excess (yang) or lacking (yin), the body, mind and spirit show signs of imbalance. The body's inner self-correcting wisdom is then triggered into action to bring the whole body back into a state of harmony. However, we, as human beings, often get in our own way and work against our inner healing wisdom by ignoring the body's signals and needs – something like ignoring the red flashing light on the car dashboard – by delaying well-needed rest periods; by overindulging in the wrong foods, the wrong exercise (or avoiding exercise); by not drinking enough water; by repressing our emotions, feelings, needs, wishes, dreams, and life purpose.

Paying attention to our body, mind and spirit, being aware of any element out of balance, and searching for possible causes for the imbalance are the best ways to regain and maintain our sense of wellness, harmony, inner peace, and happiness on all levels: physical, mental, emotional, and spiritual.

My Introduction to the Elements

Near the end of my Holistic Health Continuing Studies program, my Ayurveda instructor said something to the effect, "If you are looking to assist a client in reaching wellness balance, you need to work with the elements." Of all the interesting concepts that she had covered, this one caught my captivating attention. My question was, *"How do I do that?"*

After two years of intensive studying and completing plenty of assignments and case studies, I was looking forward to my last course for a while – *Introduction to Polarity Therapy* with Mary MacDonald, and then, a well-needed break from school. The answer to my question came 20 minutes into this last course. That night, I said to Philip, "I guess I will be going to school for another three years!"

It is in my Polarity Therapy studies with Sher Smith at *Realizing Your Potential Learning Centre* in Richmond Hill, Ontario that I became aware of the elements and began to understand how they "behave". I gained a greater appreciation of who I am and my spiritual essence, how I behave, how I get out of balance, *and* how I can get back in balance. Very empowering! I can honestly say that I feel healthier and happier, more in control of my life and better equipped to deal with life's ups and downs. Polarity has since become a part of my lifestyle. It can be the difference between *surviving* and *thriving* in a stressful life.

Sadly, Mary passed away in 2013. I miss her support and loving guidance. In memory of her influence on me, I promised to continue my studies and to share Polarity as much as possible. In my opinion, Mary and Sher are the two greatest, most inspiring pioneers of Polarity in Ontario, if not in Canada. I feel blessed and grateful to have met both of these giants. Dr. Stone, the father of Polarity Therapy, would be very proud of them!

What is Polarity Therapy?

Polarity Therapy helps you understand what is going on in your life, and the messages your body gives you. On your own or with the assistance of a Polarity practitioner, you can investigate the clues your body gives you, and then make necessary adjustments.

Dr. Randolph Stone, N.D., D.O., D.C., (1890-1981) was lauded as the father of Energy Medicine. He was a pioneer and a healer. He developed the Polarity Therapy system after fifty years of study and practice in medicine and in ancient Eastern healing systems. He named his collection of theories and techniques *"Polarity Therapy"* to describe the electromagnetic energy and beliefs underlying the Eastern health systems that include the Ayurvedic medical concepts, yogic exercises, Indian philosophy, and Traditional Chinese Medicine. He discovered that life is movement, and movement is a manifestation of *energy* or *life force,* that disease and pain occur when the natural flow of the body's energy is disrupted or blocked due to stress or other invading factors. His tireless research and life-long practice work led him to develop methods to find blockages in a patient's energy field and release held energy in order to restore the system to a higher level of health. Instead of focusing on symptoms and disease, he always looked for the health in his patient in order to "fan" it and build upon it. Therefore, Polarity Therapy became known as a "health building process". His work -- based on the principles of positive and negative energy flow within the body -- reflects his health concepts: 1) the awareness of life as energy currents that can be directly experienced through a plant-based diet and yogic exercises; 2) health encompasses all dimensions of a human being – mind, body, emotions and spirit; and 3) nourishing and expressing the soul is as important as nourishing and exercising the body. He believed that when the body is assisted in returning to its natural state of rest, relaxation and balance, its innate ability to heal is activated.

In a nut shell, Polarity Therapy is:

- A non-invasive, natural and transformational healing modality with a holistic approach; it reduces stress and promotes balance, wellness and healing;
- A way of life that leads to better health, a happier state of mind and a recollection of our origins – a reconnection with our Source;

- A tool to interpret the language of the body and to become aware of the physical symptoms as a manifestation of energy in chaos;
- It involves the five elements -- ether, air, fire, water, earth -- that are present everywhere and in everything;
- An art and a science that balance the vital life energy and the fine energy currents -- the natural electromagnetic energies -- of mind, body, spirit and soul;
- Balancing the vital life force energy and the energy currents for optimal health and wellness achieved through the following five avenues of health using the five elements as seen in Nature:
  - Time-out, stillness, meditation (ether)
  - Love; awareness of thought patterns and attitude (air)
  - Lengthening yoga exercises (fire)
  - Proper nutrition and nourishment (water)
  - Gentle hands-on bodywork and energy work (earth);
- It integrates many comprehensive healing modalities such as Ayurveda, Traditional Chinese Medicine, acupressure, yoga, essential oils, crystals, reflexology, cranio-sacral therapy, etc;
- A Polarity experience is a nourishing and nurturing process for the whole body, mind and spirit. It is a *health-building* and a *maintenance process;*
- It is about *energy*. It works with the body's energy and its innate healing abilities to facilitate rest and relaxation. Polarity Therapy allows the body to restore healthier energy flow;
- <u>Principle 1</u>: any part of the body affects the whole body.
- <u>Principle 2</u>: when working on as many layers and aspects of the body and the person, the results and the benefits tend to be greater, faster, deeper, and last longer.

The body wants to be healthy and maintain balance. It knows what to do, as long as the opportunities, the resources, the space, the time, and the guide or coach are provided. Polarity Therapy is about assisting the client to develop a greater sense of awareness, and leading the body toward a higher sense of balance.

How to Get Things Moving When You Feel *S.T.U.C.K.*

It is quite a challenge to enjoy life when you are not feeling at your best due to aches and pain, headaches, heartache, high stress level, muscle tension, relentless exhaustion, poor sleep quality, feeling overwhelmed, overweight, depressed, etc. And that is just what is going on in your body! What about dealing with work stresses and life challenges? And family responsibilities? Everything feels like a huge chore that drains the energies you have left.

Following are **9 health-building blocks** to help you construct a more solid and steady health foundation so you can be the best possible version of *you*. They form what I call my "**Nourishment Therapy**". They are designed to be part of a balanced and healthy lifestyle to help you feel better, and return to a state of greater flow and wellness. I personally use these building blocks in my life. I had to learn efficient ways to cope with emotional stress, heartache, inexplicable aches and pain, and chronic low energy. These building blocks have made a huge difference in my wellness. They gave me the strength to make positive life and career changes. I teach my clients the simple and effective techniques that you will learn in the following pages. For optimal results, I recommend that they be mindfully practiced on a regular basis.

In my practice, the clients who use these building blocks report a combination of the following benefits:

- a significant shift in their energy level;
- a clearer mind;
- a more positive outlook on life and a new sense of direction;
- a lighter feeling in their body;
- improved sleep;
- better digestion;
- decreasing weight;
- aches and pain that are significantly reduced or even eliminated;
- greater ability to deal with the stressors at home and at work;
- a strong desire to live a more meaningful life by developing new dreams and taking steps to achieve them.

Energy surrounds and permeates the planet Earth in layers of different qualities and densities. Let's start with the lightest element: **Ether**. Unlike the other four elements, Ether is not related to a zodiac sign.

Ether Characteristics	Space, stillness, rest, time-out, meditation, quiet time, the element of *being (vs. doing)*, clarity, beauty, harmony, life purpose, mission, freedom, self-expression, spirit, connection with the Universe or the Divine (the Source), universal love. It also relates to the freshness of the food and the ambiance that surrounds a meal. A space for the other 4 elements to mix.
Nature	Seashore; mountain top; any peaceful, beautiful, open and natural setting where there is a lot of great energy.
Colour	Blue
Crystal	Clear quartz
Personality	Can be spacey, dreamer, rarely manifests his dreams; feeling of "not-belonging" here on earth; claustrophobic; no purpose or too many; feeling of having no choice.
Emotions	Grief (an emotion arising from feeling separated from the Source or God); humility.
Mind	Peace, tranquillity, stillness; awareness and appreciation of esthetics and the beauty in nature.
Body	Delicately built, frail-looking with far-away look in the eye; clumsy, accident-prone; noisy, sensitive to loud noise. Ether governs all spaces in the body, joints, throat, ears, and the sense of hearing.
Communication	Difficulty in speaking and listening; soft voice; lack of self-esteem and confidence; learning disabilities; having no boundaries.
Nutrition	Attractive food presentation, fresh food with a variety of colours, tastes and textures. Sprouts, eggs.
How to get in touch with Ether and create your spa experience	• Daily meditation (taking time to be still), or a fully mentally-absorbing task of creativity such as gardening, crafts, etc. Allow yourself to take in all sights and sensations. • Prepare a colourful meal with fresh ingredients. Use your best china, fresh flowers, candles, music. Relax, and take your time to enjoy the experience and all the sensations. Become aware of how it makes you feel and how your body responds. • Spend some time in nature. Become aware of all your senses. Close your eyes and allow your ears to pick up the sounds around you. Notice how many of these sounds are natural, i.e., birds singing, tree leaves moving in the wind, water flowing? How many are human made? • Become aware of the space in your life. When do you feel there is not enough space or when do you have too much? Or just enough? How do you feel about open spaces? Confined spaces? • Have you found your life purpose? Are you able to fulfill it? • Hold your thumb or big toes (they are related to the Ether element) until you feel a buzz.

We all need solitude from time to time, to reflect on who we are, where we are, why we are here, and where we are going.

The Air Element (Zodiac Signs: Gemini, Aquarius, Libra)

Air Characteristics	Movement through physical activities to activate changes; ease of movement; mental activity, attention, thought process; changeability; planning; breathing; awareness; consciousness; mental clarity; objectivity; observation; synthesis; curiosity.
Nature	The wind, the speed of air
Colour	Green
Crystal	Amethyst
Personality	Likes mental challenges, lives in his/her head; emotionally detached; quick wit; moves from one idea to another like a butterfly; difficult to pin down, flighty nature; procrastinates.
Emotions	Desire, contentment
Mind	Great thinking abilities, quick, alert, inventive mind, indecisiveness, great sense of humour.
Body	Can be light, tall, thin, wiry, graceful; often considered a "type A" personality, anxious, nervous, fearful, talkative. Air governs all movement in the body: heartbeat, pulse, breathing, passage of food through the body, impulses of nervous system, vibration of every cell, sleep. Air allows large movement capabilities required in all physical activities. Air governs shoulders, kidneys, feet, and the sense of touch.
Communication	Loves to talk, rapid speech, constantly changes his mind.
Nutrition	Food that grows from 6 feet above the ground: fruits, nuts, citrus. Poultry; sour-tasting food: yogurt, cheese, fermented foods.
How to get in touch with Air and create your spa experience	• When you feel stuck, you need to get things moving again. A change of scenery and stimulus, or reading an exciting fiction book to stimulate the mind and imagination will create a break from the habitual thought patterns. • Breathing exercises. • Have a short nap: you may wake up with new ideas. • Dance, Tai Chi, Yoga, Qi Gong. • Go outside on a windy day and notice the effect on your body, mind, and emotions. Breathe in the fresh air. • Pick up a lemon, grapefruit, lime or orange. Close your eyes and gently rub its skin with your index finger. Smell its fragrance and imagine what its juices, its texture and its taste will be like when you cut this fruit for a salad or a juice. Cut the fruit and enjoy its segments or drink its juice in a glass of water. • Hold your index finger or 2nd toes (the are related to the Air element) until you feel a buzz.

The Fire Element (Zodiac Signs: Leo, Aries, Sagittarius)

Fire Characteristics	Intelligence, quickness of mind, insight, vitality, enthusiasm, energy, warmth of body, direction of movement, willpower, energy coming into form, focus, action, passion, self-confidence, intensity, spontaneity, optimism, authentic power, redirecting energies where they need to go, the element of *doing (vs. being)*.
Nature	The sun, a volcano, a camp fire or a fire place, a hot spring, a sauna
Colour	Gold
Crystal	Citrine
Personality	Great creative abilities, out-going, decisive, leader, risk-taker, assertive, confident, warm, sunny disposition, enthusiastic, energetic, goal-oriented.
Emotions	Anger, forgiveness
Mind	Alertness, intelligence, vitality of the eyes, direction, purposefulness, decisiveness, the need to create.
Body	May be of medium height and build; strong. Fire governs the digestive system, solar plexus, thighs, eyes, and the sense of sight.
Communication	Outspoken, honest, direct, precise speech, loud voice; can be a bully.
Nutrition	Food that grow 12 inches to 6 feet above the earth: beans, grains, seeds, bitter green vegetables and herbs, garlic, chili pepper, leeks, onion, ginger, many spices; coffee, tea, alcohol.
How to get in touch with Fire and create your spa experience	• Sit in the sun for a few minutes. Let its warm light and energy envelop you. • Sit by a fire place. • Have a physical workout to activate your muscles, energize your body and increase your internal fire. • Enjoy a handful of sunflower or pumpkin seeds. Enjoy a cup of hot ginger tea. Cook a meal with hot spices, onion, garlic and ginger like a Thai dish. Refer to this volume or Volume 1 for recipe ideas. • Hold your middle finger or 3rd toes (they are related to the Fire element) until you feel a buzz.

The Water Element (Zodiac Signs: Cancer, Scorpio, Pisces)

Water Characteristics	Intuition, flow, creativity, receptivity, nurturance, procreation, unconscious emotions, empathy, sensitivity, nourishment, cleansing, clearing.
Nature	Any body of clean, live water: sea, lake, river, waterfall, fountain
Colour	Orange
Crystal	Rose quartz
Personality	Tends to relate to the world through his/her emotions and feelings; the heart rules the head; very sensitive and intuitive, compassionate, flexible and can easily change his/her mind.
Emotions	Attachment, detachment
Mind	Connected to memory capability; can be too emotional to function properly, or operates from the head and doesn't listen to the heart.
Body	May have a moderate to stout build, a padded look. Water governs the lymph, urine, sweat, blood, mucus; chest, pelvis, feet, and the sense of taste.
Communication	Can be quite talkative, very persuasive, compassionate, constantly trying to please others or seeking approval, can be whiny.
Nutrition	Food that grow from 1 to 12 inches above the earth: green vegetables, melons, squashes, broccoli, cauliflower; fish and seafood; dairy products.
How to get in touch with Water and create your spa experience	• Get in touch with your emotions. Listen to your speech when asked about your opinions: do you answer from your head or your feelings? If emotions come up to your awareness, explore what brought them up, what needs you have that have not been met. • Keep a journal by your bed to record your dreams. • Whenever possible, spend some time near water places: lake, seashore, river, a fountain, etc. • Have a bath and feel the warm water envelop your body; or a shower and feel the water raining on you. • Give your feet regular massages to work out the tension and sore spots. • To free your pelvis, try the hula hoop, or belly dancing. Move your pelvis and hips clockwise, counter-clockwise, and in a figure 8 pattern. • Prepare a dish you thoroughly enjoy. Savour every mouthful very slowly by allowing your saliva to completely coat the food particles. • Do an activity that nourishes you physically, mentally, emotionally or spiritually. • Hold your ring finger or 4th toes (they are related to the Water element) until you feel a buzz.

The densest element: Earth (Zodiac Signs: Taurus, Virgo, Capricorn)

Earth Characteristics	Foundation, manifestation, support, stability, structure, practicality, realism, endurance, materialism, persistence, organization, safety, survival, basic needs, grounded-ness, centeredness, completion, courage.
Nature	A vegetable garden, an agricultural farm, a construction site
Colour	Red
Crystal	Smoky quartz
Personality	Can be very ambitious, a good provider, helpful, grounded; can be stubborn, nitpicking, preoccupied with basic needs; loves food; energetic to get the job done.
Emotions	Fear and courage
Mind	Earth rules the assimilation and elimination in the mind about new information and old ideas; can be a hoarder, an accumulator of facts.
Body	Can be square-looking, strong, big-boned, slow moving and talking. Earth governs structure, absorption, assimilation; colon, knees, neck, and the sense of smell.
Communication	Slow, deep voice; takes time to assimilate information and carefully considers responses which can add weight and authority to a conversation.
Nutrition	Food that grow below the ground: carrots, beets, potatoes, yams, all roots and tubers; red meat, sweeteners (honey, maple syrup, coconut sugar)
How to get in touch with Earth and create your spa experience	• Gardening, digging the soil: very grounding. • Dancing to drum music or tribal beat. • Spend some time in nature, stand or sit still, connect with the ground beneath your feet. Observe the plants, the animals, the insects. Listen to the various sounds. Feel the wind around your body. Notice if there are any smells around you. Allow your whole being to become part of this experience in nature. • Get sensual: indulge in a good meal; have a massage or a warm aromatic bath. Indulge in any activity that appeals to and stimulates your senses. • Treat yourself to a session of bodywork (aromatherapy massage, reflexology, etc.) or energy work (polarity therapy, reiki, chakra balancing, etc.). • Hold your baby finger or your baby toes (they are related to the Earth element) until you feel a buzz.

In periods of high stress, what helps me become calmer, more grounded, and think more clearly is drinking water, breathing deeply and going out for a walk.

You may recognize aspects of yourself in many of the personality characteristics of these elements. Your mind, body and spirit consist of a combination of all the elements. As a human being, you are a very complex and unique wonder with your own elemental forces. Living life to the fullest requires that you get to know yourself, accept, honour and celebrate the Divine creation that you are. It is important to recognize which elements you are happy and comfortable in, and which ones you shy away from because they feel unfamiliar or uncomfortable. All the elements are at play in your life; they enrich your experiences by offering variety and depth. All you need to do is keep them in a healthy balance so you enjoy "being in your elements".

An elemental imbalance can manifest in many ways. Here are a few examples: aches and discomfort in various parts of the body (especially the areas mentioned in the **Body** category in your zodiac sign table above), overeating, not wanting to exercise, feeling out of control, making wrong choices. When you become aware that an element is out of balance, refer to the above tables, and start shifting the energy or vibration by connecting with that element in nature, eating some food containing that energy, wearing the associated colour, and doing an activity from the related **How to get in touch with** section. Ideally, we should be able to tune into the situation of the moment and shift from one element to another. You can book a session with a Polarity practitioner. To find a Board Certified Polarity Practitioner or a Polarity Therapy training program near you, visit www.polaritytherapy.org., www.polaritytherapy.ca (Ontario and Canada), and www.realizingyourpotential.ca.

You can also spend some time with someone who is displaying the energetic qualities that you need. How will you know if a person has those qualities? Find their zodiac sign, and refer to the positive aspects of the **Characteristics, Personality** and **Mind** descriptions above. For example, if you can't get the inspiration and the creative ideas to complete a task, requesting the assistance of an Air personality (Gemini, Aquarius or Libra) might be what you need.

Health-building Block #2
Elemental Assistance
How to get the nourishment and the support that you need from the elements

How many times have you found yourself (or someone you know) in this situation: you have a project to complete by a certain date and you can't start working on it – you just can't get in the mood, you are lacking inspiration and motivation. Instead, procrastination, frustration and anxiety rule. You feel stuck!

Here is a suggestion that may help you (or the student in your household) start and successfully accomplish what needs to be done. It is a matter of rebalancing the energies that are in a yin (lacking) or in a yang (in excess) state for optimal wellness, harmony, and success. It may help improve your performance by lessening the feelings of tension and frustration, and the need to compensate with unwise food choices and unhealthy behaviours. The key words related to each element are underlined.

1. **Ether:** Being the lightest energy, everything starts with this element before manifesting in physical form. It is about space and purpose. I invite you to start becoming aware of the need to complete this project by bringing it into your life; welcoming and embracing it *versus* rejecting and resisting it. (Have you heard that "what you resist persists"?) Make it your purpose, your mission. Then, envision in your mind creating a space for this project; visualize creating a space in your home or workplace to work on it; imagine carving blocks of time in your schedule to devote mindful energies towards its completion – what you focus on expands. Take some time to sit with this vision in your mind, breathe, and allow the project to enter your being. You may need to do this a few times if your feelings around the project are not very positive! In your own way, connect with Spirit and the Source of all things. Know that you will be given the energy, the inspiration, the motivation and the resources that you need to complete this project successfully. They are all in and around you. All is needed is to connect with them. As you embrace this project, allow the energies, the inspiration and the resources to come to your awareness.

2. **Air:** Become aware of the thoughts and the beliefs that you have about this project. What statements do you often repeat to yourself? To complete this project successfully, what do you need to say to yourself? What statements and affirmations would be more supportive, uplifting and success-promoting? Notice how your energy is shifting and moving upward. Take a few deep belly breaths. If possible, go outside and breathe in some fresh air to clear your mind. Once you have cleared your mind and oxygenated your brain, it is time to plan. State your intention. Brain-storm alone or with someone (sometimes hearing a child's perspective can be inspiring) for ideas that you record on paper or in the computer: strategy, steps to take, material and resources needed, blocks of time per day/week, a new routine, anything you need to get in the process. Do you feel that things are starting to move? Do you feel the beginning of a momentum? Notice how you feel now. Also, plan a reward to be enjoyed after the project is done. It is a great motivator!

3. **Fire:** Clarify your vision of the project. And, it is time to take action, direct the energies; get focused, motivated and all fired up! If needed, talk to someone who can inspire you and ignite the driving fire inside of you to get going. Throughout the process, keep your eyes on the plan and the end result. Adjust the direction if needed. Remember the reward!

4. **Water:** It's time to get a flow going, and stay in the flow. Let the flow and the new routine that you created in the Air stage carry you to completion. Be persistent. Allow your inspired creativity and intuition to come through and make your project unique, and of great quality and value. Remember to properly nourish and hydrate yourself as food and water are needed for brain power. Enjoy the journey.

5. **Earth:** It is about structure, organization, editing, proofing, polishing. Have courage and trust in your abilities that you can reach completion of the project. You are so close to the finish line! If needed, find people who can offer you support and grounded-ness to go the distance. Once the project is completed, anchor that wonderful and joyous feeling of accomplishment in your being so your cells remember this new rewiring for the next big challenge. Reward yourself and celebrate! You deserve it! Well Done! You just created a project the elemental way! How does that feel?

Health-building Block #3
The Release of the Tendon Guard Reflex (TGR)
An effective technique to relax, release tension, manage stress and restore balance

(Adapted with permission from Sher Smith's article *The Tendon Guard Reflex and Postural Ease* published in Brain Gym® Journal – March 2006. Sher is a Registered Nurse, a Board Certified Polarity Practitioner and Educator, a Registered Cranio-sacral Therapist, and an Educational Kinesiology teacher for Brain Gym. She is the founder and director of Realizing Your Potential Learning Centre in Richmond Hill, Ontario.)

The Tendon Guard Reflex, coined by Dr. Carla Hannaford, also known as the Shock Reflex, is an unconscious response by the body to messages transmitted by the back brain or brain stem. This is the oldest part of the brain responsible for survival instincts and reflexes; it is believed to have evolved from the time when people were under constant physical stress of fighting for survival.

When the body encounters a real or perceived threat, this reflex automatically activates and causes the tendons at the back of the ankles to contract. The purpose of the tendons contracting is to hold us back until we are neurologically organized and we feel it is safe to take flight or stand and fight. The TGR serves the dual purpose of 1) preparing the body to stand and fight or turn in flight, and 2) protecting the legs to enable them to perform efficiently regardless of the action (fight or flight) chosen.

Although today these same survival needs may not be physically present, other forms of stress remain, which can and do trigger the TGR response. The dilemma in today's society is that there is often so much stress in people's lives that the TGR can be constantly over-simulated and remain locked in the contracted or stressed position without a person's conscious awareness.

Although, at first, this may seem like a small occurrence, it has significant systemic ramifications. When the tendons at the back of the ankles tighten, a chain of events occur in the body:

- the muscles of the lower legs contract, resulting in
- the tendons at the back of the knees contracting, resulting in
- the knees locking, resulting in
- the muscles, fascia and connective tissues of the upper legs and thighs contracting, resulting in
- the lower back tensing and contracting, resulting in
- the whole spine becoming stressed, resulting in
- the neck muscles becoming tightened and shortened, resulting in
- the head being pulled back.

For efficient functioning of the vestibular system, which keeps a person balanced, the eyes must remain parallel to the ground. When the neck muscles tighten and shorten, the head is tilted back triggering a counter reflex – the Oculomotor Reflex – which exerts a counter pressure through the muscles of the TMJ (temporal-mandibular jaw joints) to assist the return of the head to its proper position. This impacts the vestibular system which is directly related to the ease of learning. Having a balanced TGR enhances the system's ability to sustain attention and comprehend meaning – two vital aspects of learning and performance. From one neurological response, the whole body's physiology becomes involved – from the top to the bottom and back again. This systemic pattern can be worked on in a Polarity Therapy session or by following the instructions below.

In the field of Educational Kinesiology, Dr. Carla Hannaford discusses in her book *Smart Moves** the far reaching effects of releasing the TGR. She gives examples of working with school age children who were not talking and, after the release of the TGR, started to talk. Many children with learning difficulties are often toe walkers. When the TGR is released, they start to walk normally and their disabilities improve. Dr. Hannaford teaches parents how to apply pressure to the tendons to release them; she also encourages the parents to flex and extend the feet of the child while he or she is asleep. Encouraging results have been noted following the use of this simple technique.

A Polarity session often begins with work on the TGR. It is quite impressive to hear clients vocalize the benefits they feel from the work done on their tendons: some immediately report their TMJ muscles relaxing, and many times, realizing that they were unaware of the tightness before the stress-releasing TGR sequence started. Or, they may state that they became aware of their lower back, knees, neck or the area between their shoulder blades. Often times, they

---

* Please refer to the References and Recommended Reading section for the reference.

will release a deep sigh as their whole system begins to relax, release and unwind. This simple application has such a wide systemic influence.

Following are the instructions to perform the stress-releasing TGR sequence. You can assist a loved one who is under a lot of stress or tension feel a whole lot better very fast. You can also show your spouse or teenager how to do it on you so you, too, can enjoy the benefits of feeling lighter, calmer, and better equipped to carry on with your responsibilities. It will not remove the stressors in your life. However, the lighter, more focused and grounded energies you may experience following a TGR session can help you feel, behave and perform better. When we feel better, behave better and perform better, the whole world seems to go right(er)! We feel more in control and better able to achieve the results we want.

Instructions for the release of the TGR

This technique is often to the body system what a valve is to a pressure cooker. It benefits cases of speech problems and learning difficulties, chronic fatigue, tension headache, tense and tight muscles, TMJ, tinnitus, constipation. It promotes relaxation and the release of stress in the connective tissues. Please read all the instructions before starting.

1. Create a sacred space where you won't be disturbed so the person (or "the client") can feel safe to unwind, release tension, and let go. Have the person lie down on their back on a bed or a massage table, with a pillow or cushion under the knees and another one under the head. Bring a chair or a stool near the foot of the bed for you to sit on.
2. Ask your client how they are feeling, what they notice in their body. Ask your client how they would like to feel after this technique. Invite your client to take a deep belly breath: a long and deep inhalation from the chest and belly, a pause, a long and complete exhalation, followed by a pause. Repeat several times.
3. Place the tips of your fingers on the Achilles tendon of each ankle of your client. (The Achilles tendon is a band of hard tissues located between the heel and below the calf muscles on the back of the leg.) If your nails are long, you may have to clip them for your client's comfort. Within the client's tolerance, apply a firm pressure on the tendons upward, toward the front of the legs.
4. While applying the pressure on the tendons, keep your thumbs on the lateral side of the ankle; **do not squeeze the ankles.** Encourage your client to breathe deeply, relax and let go of any tension. Groaning and sighing loudly while exhaling is quite all right. As a matter of fact, sound often assists the movement of stuck energy.
5. Keep pressing on the Achilles tendons until your client appears more relaxed, breathes deeply, and the tissues under your fingers feel softened and more flexible. This may take several minutes, so take deep breaths and relax, too.
6. During the session, you may notice that the client's legs or body start to tremor as excess energy in the tissues is being released – this is normal.
7. After applying pressure to the tendons, you can flex and extend the feet to bring more release.
8. Massage the two baby toes simultaneously, and hold them gently between your thumbs, index and middle fingers for a few minutes. Do the same with each of the other toes, finishing with the big toes. This step helps balance the elemental energies in the whole body.
9. Invite the client, when they are ready, to turn on their side and slowly sit up. When ready, they can slowly get up and take a few steps. Ask them how they feel and what they notice is different in their body. Give them a glass of water to drink and tell them to rest for a while.

I highly recommend that you teach this effective technique to a family member or a friend so you, too, can receive its benefits. I taught Philip how to do it and he is more than happy to give me a session whenever I have a migraine headache or I feel tired, tensed, stressed out, worried, over-analyzing, restless, and even sore. Sometimes he will even offer it when he notices that I am not comfortable or that I am becoming less adorable! This simple technique works wonders: I always feel much better once I get up from the massage table. In fact, after several hours of gardening or other physically-demanding chores that make me ache all over, I found that within a few minutes after receiving a TGR session, I am much more flexible and comfortable in my body. It saves me days of suffering from overall stiffness and sore muscles.

"Tension is who you think you should be. Relaxation is who you are."
-Old Chinese proverb

Health-building Block #4
Dr. Stone's Purifying Diet
A gentle internal spring cleaning to detox, recharge and get you on the path to wellness

Adapted from Franklyn Sills' book *The Polarity Process, Energy as a Healing Art** and from Sher Smith's *Polarity Therapy Certification Training Manual**.

Dr. Stone used naturopathic dietary principles and procedures for internal cleansing and health building. Due to imbalances in body function, to poor diet and to pollutants, the detoxification and eliminative organs become overloaded, and toxic wastes accumulate in the body tissues. He developed a cleansing diet that consists of a morning "liver flush" to help with the detoxification, and a nutrition plan of vegetables and fruit in mostly raw form to aid the eliminative process. A cleansing tea is also taken throughout the day. The herbs and seeds can be found at regular grocery stores and herbal stores.

This Purifying Diet is helpful in cases of constipation, high blood pressure, arthritis, pain, swelling, congestion, toxicity, excess weight, and as a general cleanser for three to seven days in a row three or four times a year – or once per season. Or when you start feeling sluggish and not your usual self.

In my wellness practice, I recommend this cleanse to my clients who complain of not feeling well, are under a lot of stress, have poor sleep quality, are experiencing aches and pains, inflamed joints, etc. It is best to do the cleanse during a weekend so you have more time to rest and prepare your meals. Those who have tried it have reported feeling much better by the third day with lots of energy, a clearer mind, and a general lighter feeling. Unfortunately, shortly after the purifying process, most people go back to their bad habits, "retox" and notice the reappearance of their symptoms.

There are 2 different drinks to prepare: 1) a **Liver Flush Herb Tea**, and 2) a **Liver Flush Drink**.

Most of the ingredients for the **Herb Tea Mixture** and the **Liver Flush Drink** can be purchased separately at most grocery stores. You can find the licorice root at herbal stores or order on-line.

Please note: The Herb Tea Mixture is contraindicated in case of pregnancy.

1st step:
Liver Flush Herb Tea

Prepare this **Herb Tea** first so it will be ready for drinking immediately
following the **Liver Flush Drink in 2nd step**.

4 slices gingerroot, cut in ¼ inch thick 3 cups of filtered water	**Herb Tea Mixture**: 1 tsp licorice root 1 tsp peppermint leaves 1 tsp fenugreek seeds 1 tsp fennel seeds 1 tsp flaxseeds

In a non-aluminum pot, boil the gingerroot slices in 3 cups of water for 3 minutes.
Turn the heat down, and add the **Herb Tea Mixture**.
Cover and simmer for 10-15 minutes. While the tea is steeping, prepare the **Liver Flush Drink.**

2nd step:
Liver Flush Drink

In a blender, mix together:

the juice of 1 grapefruit or 1-2 oranges 6 tbsp fresh lemon juice 3 tbsp cold-pressed olive oil	**Optional:** 1 garlic clove, crushed, and a dash of cayenne pepper

Directions for the Purifying Diet:

1. Drink this frothy Liver Flush Drink (2nd Step). Then, drink a cup of the Liver Flush Herb Tea (1st Step) while it is hot.
2. During the day, drink as many cups of the Liver Flush Tea as possible.

---

* Please refer to the References and Recommended Reading section for the reference.

3. One hour or two later, drink some fresh citrus juice or other fresh fruit juice (apples, pears, grapes, etc.) or some fresh vegetable juice (a blend of carrot, cabbage, celery, beet, etc.)

4. For lunch, eat plenty of leafy green and other vegetables such as lettuce, carrots, turnips, squash, spinach, leeks, celery, cabbage, broccoli, cauliflower, string beans, radishes, cucumbers, beets, and sprouts: alfalfa, fenugreek, mung beans, lentils. You can make a dressing with lemon juice, honey, extra-virgin olive oil, garlic, ginger, etc. You can refer to the **Loading Up on Greens -- Vegetables and Side Dishes** section in this book and in **Volume 1** for more suggestions. Eat the vegetables in raw form as much as possible, but you may also steam, bake, or make them into soups. *Do not fry them!*

5. For dessert, you may eat fresh fruits such as apples, pears, grapes, peaches, fresh berries. You can also eat soaked prunes and dried figs.

6. A moderate amount of raw almonds may be eaten.

7. If you are still hungry, you can have baked or steamed vegetables or a cup of warm vegetable broth. See **While Waiting for the Next Meal – Snacks and Beverages** section for dairy-free ideas.

8. For an afternoon snack, you can have a glass of fresh vegetable juice.

9. For dinner, have a fruit and herbal tea. If you are still hungry, have a salad.

10. To finish the day, brush your skin dry with a loofah brush and have a warm bath. Before bed, do some gentle yoga poses and light reading.

11. During this Purifying diet, **do not eat** meat, fish, chicken, eggs, starches (potatoes, rice, bread, cereal), sugar (however, honey and maple syrup are permissible), milk or milk products, coffee, regular tea, alcohol, unnecessary drugs -- not even aspirin. **Check with your doctor first!** Do not use aluminum cookware.

12. Beware that before you experience enhanced energy and a general lighter feeling in your body, detox symptoms may appear as your body releases toxins. The discomfort is temporary. You **may** experience some of the following detox symptoms:
    - Headache and nausea
    - Vomiting
    - Tiredness, lethargy, drowsiness or dizziness
    - Mucus discharge (runny nose, phlegm), flu-like symptoms
    - Skin eruption
    - Improved bowel movement and bladder function
    - Deep relaxation (you may feel tired, sleepy for a day or two)
    - Cold or flushed feeling or a fever
    - Flatulence
    - Perspiration
    - Aches and pains
    - Bad taste or dryness in the mouth
    - Watery eyes
    - Rush of emotional release, mild mood swings
    - Revitalized or energized
    - Emotional release, giggles

13. Drink lots of purified water to flush out the toxins – at least 8 glasses. You may add a few lemon slices in the water.

14. Get as much rest, relaxation and sleep as possible. Take a warm bath; sip a warm cup of peppermint or chamomile tea.

15. Detoxifying and healing take place on several levels of the being: physical, mental, emotional and spiritual. You might want to write or journal about the emotions that surface, and the wonderful self-discoveries you may experience during this purifying process. With clearer thoughts, you might be able to envision new dreams, goals and wishes for yourself and your loved ones.

16. If the weather permits it, spend some time walking or sitting outdoors in the sun and fresh air. Enjoy the scenery and connect with the five natural elements: earth, water (if present), fire (the sun), air, ether (nature's beauty, space, freshness).

17. Above all, listen to your body. Nurture and pamper yourself: you need and deserve it. It is not self-indulgence; it is *a necessity* if you want to live a long, healthy and vibrant life in today's world. Enjoy the journey!

C- Developing Your Own "EMaSC" Ritual –
Your Everyday Mediter-asian Spa Care Ritual –
for Relaxation, Stress Management and Wellness

There is a peaceful sanctuary within you
where you can take refuge and be yourself.

To feel better and be healthy, incorporating restorative, cleansing, and healing rituals in your everyday living is more a necessity than a luxury. Giving yourself permission to take time to care and nurture yourself is possibly one of the greatest acts of self-love that will have many expected and unexpected, subtle and more profound benefits for you and your loved ones, in all areas of your life. The enhanced sense of wellness, harmony and inner beauty may just give you a self-confidence boost and passionate drive to start living your dreams and making an even more impactful difference in your corner of the world. As you transform yourself and your life, it is bound to create a rippling effect all around you. You could be the pebble in your pond. I invite you to visit my website www.olivestolychees.com for a free copy of my e-book on personal transformation *The REAL YOU: Your Gift to the World*.

Sometimes the best thing to do is to rest.

Your own "EMaSC" ritual is about enhancing your body's ability to recharge and heal itself by tapping into its health-building potential. Your natural healing ritual is about re-awakening your senses to the benefits of regularly taking time out to experience the 5 Rs: Rest, Relaxation, Repair/Recharge, Rejuvenation, and Re-creation.

Saying "No" Can Be Liberating -- Saving You Time and Energy

It is so easy to get caught up in work deadlines, overwhelming requests and "favours", as well as time-consuming social-familial priorities. We are so well trained to push ahead to meet external commitments and responsibilities that we keep on delaying our internal needs like making time for restful pauses, adequate sleep, proper nourishment and hydration, stress-reducing exercises. I know this behaviour very well; I catch myself in that mode, too. Like many of you, I am a people pleaser and I like to help. As a result, I can easily get out of balance trying to do it all. Luckily, my body's wisdom overrides my mind's agenda and lets me know *very clearly* that it is not happy with my "overdoing it" and threatens to make me even more miserable if I continue to neglect its needs. Therefore, when possible, before I get too overwhelmed, resentful and incapacitated from a stress overload, I slow down and "retreat" by saying "No, thank you!" to extra demands I don't feel up to fulfilling; then, I withdraw for a period of rest and reflection to recharge. It is not always easy, but I am getting better at it. I don't feel as guilty any more, nor do I feel the need to justify why I don't want to sacrifice my precious time and energy. Resentment doesn't make anyone happy. Prevention and regular maintenance are always wiser and cheaper than treatments and cures.

I have learned to evaluate my "Yeses" and my "Nos" in relation to extra demands and what I am willing to give of myself. Before accepting to fulfill a request, I quickly run the following questions through my head: What will the consequences be if I don't fulfill this request? Am I the best person to handle this request? Do I *really* want to fulfill it? What will my energetic cost be, and is it possible for me to get the rest I need after? Will fulfilling this request require that I spend time away from Philip?

"We know so much about disease, but nothing about health!
Don't treat disease; treat the individual. Find out where the energy is blocked!"
-Dr. Randolph Stone, *Health Building, a Conscious Art of Living Well*

Finding the Root Cause of Ailments by Being Self-aware

Ailments occur when the repair and healing processes can't keep up with the damage process. Being self-aware and observant are two qualities essential to optimal wellness. We must slow down, stop and take regular rest before overwhelming fatigue and illness bring us down. What matters is what we do on a regular basis between visits to the doctor; not so much when we occasionally transgress. It is when we are not supervised or held accountable that we need to learn to be wise, listen to our body and respect its signals and clues rather than ignore, numb or medicate them. The signals, clues and symptoms are messages from the body letting us know that something needs to change, and not necessarily on the physical level. Our health, expressed through our body, is a mirror of our life. Our body will react when an aspect (mental, emotional, physical or spiritual) of our life is out of balance and needs attention. The body's unique way to communicate and express itself is often through some discomfort – skin rash, inexplicable pain, stiffness -- as the first layer into the real issue. If we ignore the communication from the body, the signals will become louder, more intense and more painful. The root cause of the symptoms often lies in the way we live our lives, how we treat ourselves, what we think about and believe in. We need to notice and understand what makes us uncomfortable in our lives, what is going against our nature.

The key to wellness is to take time to tune in to our bodies, notice what is going on, and recognize that the signs contain messages. Wellness is about being willing to care for ourselves as a way to respect the amazingly beautiful divine creation that the body is, and to prevent illness instead of taking the body for granted and then, when a medical issue surfaces, attempt to find a quick fix so we can get back to our routines. Focusing only on symptom treatment doesn't offer long-term solution. Finding the root causes of ailments and illnesses requires courage, love, dedication and patience to understand what the body is trying to bring to the surface. Root causes of ailments can be so obvious and painful that it is very challenging to face them (for example, someone who is living in a very cluttered house may be experiencing blocked arteries; someone else who can't let go of past emotional hurt can experience a number of health issues). Or, they can be so subtle that you need the assistance of a supportive and skilled practitioner to help you "excavate" – or peel the layers as you would an onion -- into your self to find out the reason(s) and the moment when you lost yourself, your true essence, your highly-spirited energetic self.

Unlike any attempts to fix health problems, this excavation, done solo or with assistance, very often leads to priceless self-discoveries, significant shifts and amazing healing solutions. The healing journey can reveal hidden strengths and weaknesses, as well as an urgent call to find your way back to your true self again. When we take the time to understand the messages from the body and make the necessary changes in our lifestyle, our behaviour, our thoughts and beliefs, the symptoms often disappear. Health and healing are not necessarily about the absence or the disappearance of physical symptoms. They are more about discovering -- or renewing -- a sense of purpose and meaning to our life, as well as feeling inner ease and peace.

"We want to dominate and tell God what to do – after misusing what He gave us…
I used to run the universe, and then I got out of it. Now it runs better!"
-Dr. Randolph Stone, founder of Polarity Therapy, *Health Building, a Conscious Art of Living Well*

An Invitation to Renew Yourself

In this part of the book, you will find an invitation to set aside your worries, commitments and responsibilities to be in the present moment. It is an invitation to renew yourself and gently bring your whole being back in balance. You are invited to become an active manager of your body's wellness and nourishment by creating a spa care ritual that works for you. Please, allow the following recipes and suggestions to inspire you to develop what will make you feel relaxed, pampered, nourished and recharged after a day's work. I will guide you to sample the easy recipes for deliciously refreshing beverages, aromatic bath salts, botanical body care products, followed by the soul-satisfying spa food that you can prepare and enjoy in your own blissful oasis.

Following are a few suggestions for stress management and relaxation that you may find beneficial to explore as part of your Spa Care Ritual. They are simple and don't require complicated or expensive material. **Please note that these suggestions do not replace the care of a professional health care practitioner or a massage therapist.** They can be practiced as a regular home self-care maintenance program between massages and holistic health sessions to unwind and remind the body what it feels like to be relaxed, recharged and rejuvenated. **If you are pregnant, breast feeding, suffering from any illness or having any concerns or questions regarding a technique or recipe presented in this book, please consult with your physician. Listen to your body, trust your awareness, and follow your good judgment.**

When you are lying in a hospital bed,
you realize that your work is secondary to your health.

Health-building Block #5
A Sensual Exercise of Stillness - Taking Time Out
to Rest, Relax and Focus on the Senses
It's time to sit back, put your feet up and catch your breath.

It is in silence and stillness that you can access your own inner light
and hear the Divine messages you have been asking for.
Still yourself, breathe, listen.

1. For optimal enjoyment and benefits -- such as increased awareness, deep relaxation, refreshed senses, and improved ability to concentrate -- you may want to first read the **Steps 1-5**, gather the material needed and have it near you so you will be able to flow from one sense to the other. You can also choose to focus on one sense only. Select items that bring you great pleasure. You will find the suggested items in **Step 4**.

2. Before this mindfulness exercise of natural relaxation, notice how you are feeling in the present moment: any tension, aches, pain, tightness in chest, shallow breathing, fast heartbeat, stress, fatigue, mental chatter, racing thoughts, etc.

3. **To prepare yourself for the mindfulness exercise**:
   a. Sit comfortably in a quiet room, with your feet up on a chair or stool, and your spine erect. You can also sit up in bed and lean against the head board. Then, spend a few minutes focusing on your breathing. Here is an example of a breathing sequence: slowly, count to 4 as you take a deep inhalation to fill your chest and belly; pause for a count of 2; slowly, count to 4 as you take a complete exhalation to release all the air from your chest and belly; and pause for a count of 2. Repeat the deep breathing sequence several times. You can adjust the counts to your comfort level, gradually making the pauses and the exhalations longer. This simple mindful breathing session helps calm the nervous system; it can be very useful when you feel anxious or restless.
   b. Allow your full awareness to focus on the sense(s) being stimulated by the item(s) that you selected. Notice and acknowledge the thoughts that cross your mind. There will be many of them, and that is normal. The human mind is programmed to envision the future and revisit the past. Without attaching any energy to them, watch your thoughts go by as you would watch clouds pass by in the sky. When you become aware that you are doing a mental "To-do List" or you are replaying an earlier conversation, gently bring your focus back to your sense(s) and the present moment. To slow down the activity in your mind and keep your thoughts from spinning or racing all over the map, you might want to repeat to yourself these simple anchoring words "Here" as you inhale deeply, and "Now" as you exhale completely. (Repeating anchoring words help bring the awareness back to the present moment and to the breath. There are other words that would uplift as well as calm your mind: "Peace", "Love", "Wellness", "Gratitude". Choose what resonates best with you.) While you continue breathing deeply, imagine that you are inhaling calmness, and exhaling stress. Do this for a few minutes.

4. Spend as much time as you like noticing what your senses are relaying to you. Keep breathing deeply as you begin the sensual exercise with the items that you chose.
   Sight Look at beautiful pictures, colourful mandalas, intricate designs. You can also use a lit candle that you place safely on a table near you. Soften your eyes so that your gaze becomes meditative. Let yourself be absorbed in the picture, the design or the glow of the flame.

Hearing Listen to nature sounds (live or on a CD), classical music or any soothing instrumental recordings. Or focus on the sound of your breathing by listening to the waves of your inhalations and exhalations washing through you.

Touch Stimulate this sense by holding in your hand a crystal (i.e., any quartz) or a semi-precious stone of your choice or a special pebble or seashell.

Smell Inhale high-quality therapeutic-grade essential oils (any citrus or coniferous oil). No oils? Simply cut open an orange, a lime or a lemon; or rub between your fingers a fresh sprig of rosemary, lavender or basil; or place a few drops of stress-reducing, happiness-producing vanilla extract on a tissue. Allow the fragrant oil particles to float to your nose, and inhale slowly and deeply several times.

Taste Sip a glass of water that has been infused with fresh mint, lemon, strawberries, orange slices, etc. Let the flavoured water linger in your mouth. Savour its refreshing quality.

Heart Connect with your heart by placing both hands on your chest. Connect with your feelings of appreciation and deep gratitude for all the wonderful people, the blessings (big and small) in your life, and your senses that allow you to experience the beauty of life. Allow these feelings of appreciation and gratitude to expand in your whole body.

Being Connect with your whole being: be thankful for your physical state, your emotional state, your mental state, your spiritual state. No judgment; just noticing. Repeat this mantra from John Lennon's song *Beautiful Boy*: "Every day in every way, it's getting better and better."

5. **To end this mindfulness exercise**: Take a minute or so to savour this peaceful moment and appreciate the effects of this exercise. Notice how much calmer and more relaxed you feel. Does your head feel clearer? Has your heart rate slowed down? Are you breathing more deeply and fully? Is there a sense of peace in and around you now? What has changed in your body? Does it feel like you just created a brand new *YOU*? You may want to record what you felt, and any insight that came through as you were clearing your mind.

It is a great preparation for a good night of sleep. It can be enjoyed after receiving a TGR session (refer to **Building Block #3**). You may want to adopt this calming stillness exercise as a part of your regular wellness ritual, and vary the items to keep it interesting. After several repetitions, you may notice that you feel more peaceful and serene, your blood pressure and heart rate are lower, your mind is more focused but relaxed, it is easier to concentrate, and your self-awareness and noticing skills have improved. You may also notice that you are better able to cope with stress. This sensual exercise of stillness is very portable and can be performed on a plane, on a bus, at your work desk during a break, while waiting for an appointment, etc. Just focus on the senses that require simple items that you have on hand.

To find your treasure, follow your passion.

Health-building Block #6
Art as a Sacred Practice
A way to express your creative spirit, relax, manage stress and re-create. No talent or skills needed!

"When was the last time you made music?
When did you last dance?
When was the last story you told?
When was the last time you engaged in the 'work' of art?"

According to Tom Crockett, writer, artist, shamanic practitioner and author of *The Artist Inside, a Spiritual Guide to Cultivating Your Creative Self**, "these are the questions a shaman or indigenous healer might ask if you came seeking help or guidance. It wouldn't matter whether your condition was physical, emotional, or spiritual." "If your answer to any of these questions is 'not within the past six months,' you might be instructed to go home and sing, dance, perform, or express your creative spirit. This recommendation alone is often considered sufficient to cure an illness." The shaman or indigenous healer could identify the emotional or spiritual distress as growing from a lack of connection to community and spirit.

He adds that "there is a connection between artistic expression and spirit that resides deep in our ancestral

---

* Please refer to the References and Recommended Reading section for the reference.

memory. The native and indigenous cultures, from which we all descend, understand this connection. It is only our contemporary Western view of art that de-emphasizes the connection between the material and the spirit." "The tribal individual engaging in artistic expression first accesses the realm of spirit, seeking what we might call inspiration or the breath of the Divine. This Divine inspiration is then translated into material form with words, images, music, dance, or artifacts. Engaging the spirit, now in material form through ritual, completes the cycle. This ritual releases that spirit and draws artist and community alike back into sacred communion with the Divine. This is the sacred creative cycle. It is a cycle of transformation." "When art is about transformation, it is a sacred practice."

What would you like to transform in you and in your life? How would that benefit you, your loved ones, and your community? Most of us don't see ourselves as artists or even creative. We tend to downplay the little talent we feel we have. In fact, very few of us have chosen artistic expression as a career path. However, we are all good at something and we have been creating all our lives. I am inviting you to list 10 things that you are good at, 5 things that you used to do and enjoyed, 5 things you would like to do again or learn. I see this sacred practice as a fascinating activity that you pursue for your own passion, rejuvenation and personal growth, and where the main focus is centered on your pleasurable experience and "re-creation".

Your list could include the common "creative arts": painting, gardening, sewing, sculpting, drawing, photography, dancing, singing, playing music, writing, poetry, knitting, jewellery making, woodworking, etc. I bet there is something that I haven't included in this list that you do so well and for which you can develop a creative passion. Look at your list of 20 things; are there any surprises? Choose one or two creative endeavours you would like to develop as part of your Sacred Practice to nourish and express your creative spirit. What do you need to do to start and get going? You don't have to share your creations with anyone if you don't want to. However, if you don't share your creations and your process, you will not know the effect your inspiration will have on others and the happiness you will be spreading. Remember, you could be the pebble in your pond.

This sacred creative practice could be what you need to relax, clear your mind, release stress and suppressed emotions, and replenish your energies while connecting with your spiritual essence. Because it involves all aspects of your being, this sacred creative practice has a holistic effect. As you access the unconscious aspect of yourself, you might even make unexpected self-discoveries that could change your life for the better. You might heal some parts of you that need some well-deserved attention and tender loving care. *The main purpose for this ritual is to provide you with an outlet to express your emotions and your creative spirit into a form other than verbal.*

Creativity is about allowing ourselves to experiment and make mistakes. Art is about using the wisdom gained from the mistakes and repeating what works. The Art of Feeling Well is doing what works as a practice after experimenting with various relaxation and stress management techniques.

Leisure is food for the soul.

In the chapter on *Transforming your creativity* in the book *Free Your Creative Spirit**, authors Vivianne and Christopher Crowley write that "Creativity is an alchemical process. We bring together memories, dreams, sensory impressions, and skills. A synthesis occurs that produces a result – our personal alchemical gold – that is greater than the sum of the parts. Psychologists who have studied creativity and creative people agree that the creative process has four stages: preparation, incubation, illumination, and verification. If we understand these four stages, we can begin to understand our creative processes better. These four stages can be equated with the four elements of alchemy – earth, water, fire, and air."

Preparing – Earth

It involves the practical preparations, what we want to do and the materials we need. The conscious mind with left-brain activity is working on the project using the knowledge and skills we currently have.

Incubating – Water

It is the stage when we may step back from the project, to let go and stop thinking and worrying about it. When we are not consciously pursuing the problem, a new answer or solution comes in an unexpected way. When we are relaxed or sleeping, our brain continues to process ideas, events, impressions, intuition, stimulations, joys, fears of the day, etc.

---

* Please refer to the References and Recommended Reading section for the reference.

Illuminating – Fire

New ideas come to our mind like fiery lightening flash, inspirations, aha moments, especially first thing in the morning after a night's rest. A simple way to request assistance with our creative work from our unconscious mind is to light a candle before starting to work, while reminding ourselves that creative inspiration comes from a deeper source of our being than our everyday conscious mind.

Verifying – Air

It involves again our left brain and our logical rational judgment to test out the new ideas received in the previous stage and see if they can work. Once we have the illumination, we need to turn it into some creative work using our knowledge, skills, and memories of previous experiences.

Transforming – Ether, the Creative Spirit

This mysterious fifth element is both within and beyond the other four. Creativity comes from doing what must be done: expressing the creative spirit within us and not allowing it to be silenced. It is a Divine gift; it is part of our true essence.

So, get your material ready. Ground yourself and breathe deeply. Connect with your creative spirit. Listen to the Divine voice within you. Let the Divine energy flow through you … And turn that energy into form! Feeling excited already?

You are invited to visit my website www.olivestolychees.com for a free copy of my e-book on Personal Transformation: *The REAL YOU: Your Gift to the World.*

Health-building Block #7
Moving Your Body
A way to release stress, recharge and rejuvenate

Walking

a. **Brisk walk**: A 30 to 45-minute brisk walk (walking as if I am late) in the sun or on a windy day – or any day -- clears my head, recharges my batteries and oxygenates my whole body. It helps release stress in my limbs, especially if I have been sitting too long. I go out with the intention of getting some movement for my body and some inspiration for my projects. It is often during a walk that I find solutions to problems, new ideas for creative work, and a clear direction to a puzzling situation. While walking, I focus on the flowing rhythm of my feet touching the ground and my deep breathing; it feels like a meditation. After a few minutes, ideas start flashing in my head. I learned to carry in my pocket a small notepad and a pen to record the juicy inspiration. Once it feels like nothing else is coming to my awareness, I send my gratitude for the Divine guidance and enjoy the beautiful environment. I go back home refreshed, lighter, and more grounded. Please refer to **Volume 1** for other movement ideas.

b. **Slow walk**: With all your senses turned on, observe and notice as much as possible of your surroundings (nature, houses, etc.), breathe deeply and smell the fresh air, feel your feet on the ground and the rhythmic movement of your hips and arms, listen to the sounds around you (from nature and human made), feel the wind on your face and body. This type of walk is for the enjoyment of being outdoors in slow motion. The slower you walk, the more you can see, notice and appreciate.

Movement makes the body and the spirit happy.
When the body and the spirit are happy, all is well.

Soul Dancing

When undirected and free, this activity is a powerful way to help you get in touch with your feelings and release pent-up physical and emotional stress. It invites you to freely express your "flowing aquatic and earthy primitive" nature, as Chrissie Wildwood writes in *The Complete Guide to Reducing Stress**. It encourages spontaneity and the confidence to be true to yourself and others. It is about flowing with the music and becoming one with it. It is about getting out of your head, surrendering to the **spirit** of the dance, the music and the body. It is about feeling the music, losing your self in the dance, allowing the body to take over and improvise the movements. For the flowing dance, Chrissie suggests to start with a classical piece like Debussy's *Clair de Lune*, or a New Age composition with an oceanic or watery mood. For the wild and abandoned dance, she says that the ideal rhythm is fast shamanic drumming, or anything with a strong rhythmic pulse of about ninety beats per minute.

This stress release exercise is most beneficial performed barefoot outdoors in nature with like-minded soul dancers for as long as you have stamina. It is great under the moonlight – with headphones if you don't want your neighbours as witnesses! I like to hold light colourful scarves that can easily flow as I move around. If it is not possible to dance outdoors, you can let loose indoors. You can close your eyes and let your body move in any way it needs to. You may also make sounds to enhance the release of stored energy and emotions inside your body. Dr. Stone believed that expressing emotions such as crying, sighing, shouting, groaning and moaning can move stuck or repressed energy. I add laughing and singing to the list. So, put some music on, and move your feet and hips. Let loose and have fun! I know you will feel better!

> *"Rhythmic expressions of song and dance which use all the bodily forces and muscles for expression,*
> *free the emotions by naturally liberating the energy blocks, suppressions, frustrations and stagnations.*
> *And when the mind, body and emotions are used in one effort of rhythmic exercise,*
> *it becomes a triune health movement of balance."*
> -Dr. Randolph Stone, from his book <u>Health Building, a Conscious Art of Living Well</u>

Stimulating the Lymphatic System

The lymphatic system is a network of tiny vessels filled with colourless fluid that flows through the body alongside the blood. The lymph fluid is made of water and waste materials, collected from the tissues and transported in the blood to the heart to be filtered through the thousands of lymph nodes that cluster along the lymphatic vessels. Large clusters are found in the back of the knees, groin, armpits and neck areas. The major role of the lymphatic system is the body's defense against disease. By keeping the lymph moving, the body's ability to overcome infection is increased, and it is less likely to suffer from water retention and cellulite buildup. Since it is a one-way pump-less system, the lymph flows only toward the heart. To prevent waste accumulation in the lymph nodes resulting in lack of energy, sickness, and fat buildup, the lymph needs physical activity – the contracting and relaxing action of the muscles -- to function properly. Here are a few ways to assist the movement of lymph.

1. **Gentle yoga**: Not only do they help improve concentration, bring you in the present moment and maintain overall flexibility, lengthening yoga exercises and deep breathing help keep the lymph healthy and moving.
2. **Rebounding**: Jumping on a mini trampoline for about fifteen to twenty minutes to activate the lymph flow.
3. **Walking**: At a fast pace to increase breathing and blood circulation, and reverse the damage of sitting too long. Whether you are in the country or in the city, go in nature on a sunny day, if possible, at a lake, a beach or a park. Connect with the surroundings and the elements. The more pleasant the surroundings, the more beneficial and enjoyable the walk. Breathe deeply and walk for at least 45 minutes. Studies show that walking is beneficial for brain health as it increases creative output, learning and memory. It also helps reduce the risks of heart disease and hip fractures. *(The photo shows Victoria Park and the beach in Cobourg, ON where I love to walk.)*
4. **Dry skin brushing**: Before bathing or showering, with a dry skin brush, gently tap around the back of your knees, your groin and armpits where lymph nodes cluster. Then, ***gently*** brush in upward circular motion

---

* Please refer to the References and Recommended Reading section for the reference.

along your limbs from your toes to your waist, from your waist (front and back) toward your heart, from your fingers to your armpits.

5. **Aromatherapy massage:** To stimulate and detoxify the lymphatic system, blend in 1 ounce of grapeseed oil the following therapeutic-grade essential oils: 3 drops of cypress, 1 drop of orange and 2 drops of grapefruit. Massage the limbs and the torso in *gentle* circular motions toward the heart.

6. **Aromatherapy bath**: The following essential oils help stimulate and detoxify the lymphatic system: fennel, grapefruit, geranium, juniper, lavender, rosemary. Choose 3-4 therapeutic-grade oils to create a blend; then, add up to 10 drops of the oil blend to ⅓ cup of Epsom salts in the bath water. Get in the tub, relax and breathe deeply the aromatic essence. Remember to drink water.

Benefits of aromatherapy

Aromatherapy is the art and science of using essential oils to improve physical and emotional well-being. They were mankind's first medicine. They are made from flowers, fruits, leaves, roots and other parts of plants. Each essential oil provides unique therapeutic properties and exquisite fragrance or aroma. Each aroma affects the part of the brain that governs the emotions. Each oil has the potential to balance the mood, lift the spirits, dispel negative emotions, and create a sensual, romantic atmosphere. Essential oils benefit body, mind and spirit when they are inhaled, absorbed through the skin in a massage or added to bath water.

Safety precautions to keep in mind before using essential oils

Although all the ingredients used in this book are natural and considered safe, it is important to follow the safety tips listed below, especially if you are just beginning to learn about the oils:

- Since the active ingredients in any essential oil are highly concentrated, the oil should always be **diluted** in a carrier oil (vegetable oils such as grapeseed, almond, jojoba or avocado) before being applied to the skin.
- Do not ingest essential oils. Use them diluted in a carrier oil on your skin, in a bath or in a steam inhalation. Keep them out of the reach of children.
- Avoid contact with the eyes. If some of the preparation gets in your eyes, rinse immediately with warm water.
- **Skin sensitivity**: to ensure that the oil(s) you plan on using will not cause any adverse reaction, it is recommended to test your skin by dabbing a small amount of essential oil diluted in vegetable oil on the inside of your forearm below your elbow, and leaving it overnight. A skin reaction? Do not use that oil.
- **Photosensitivity**: Bergamot and citrus essential oils should NOT be applied to the skin that will be exposed to direct sunlight or ultraviolet light within 72 hours.
- **If you are under a doctor's care,** consult your physician.
- Some oils should be **avoided** in the following conditions:
  i. In the presence of **High Blood Pressure**: avoid using hyssop, rosemary, sage and thyme.
  ii. In the presence of **Epilepsy**: avoid using cedarwood, hyssop, sage, fennel and rosemary.
  iii. During **pregnancy**: avoid using aniseed, basil, bay, birch, cedarwood, citronella, clary sage, clove, geranium, hyssop, lavender, fennel, juniper berry, marjoram, peppermint, rose, rosemary, sage, thyme, wintergreen. Consult your physician.

Health-building Block #8
Nourishing Your Body with Natural Spa Care Products and Gentle "Treatments"
Relaxing, pampering and rejuvenating body and mind

If you care about what you put *in* your body, you must care about what you put *on* it as well. Therefore, the products you put on your skin should be made with natural ingredients from Mother Nature. They should be good enough to eat! They may not appeal to your taste buds but they will not make you ill. The following recipes are easy to make, and the crafted products are gentle on the body. They happen to be big sellers with my clients. I hope you enjoy them, too!

Please note:

1. **I suggest that you perform a patch test on a small area of your forearm before using your creation on a larger surface of your body.**
2. **Salt and salt water draw out impurities and toxins. They can be dehydrating. Make sure that you sip water or herbal tea as you relax.**

Home Spa Tools, Supplies and Materials

The ingredients suggested in the following recipes can be found at the grocery store and the health food store. The dried rose petals and buds can be found at the Asian food market in the tea section.

When you are ready to book some time off for well-deserved pampering, read the recipes and techniques ahead of time, and do all your shopping a few days before. You might even want to prepare some of the recipes the day before. Collect all the supplies you will need: books for pleasure reading like novels or even beautiful and healthful cookbooks; CDs of nature recordings or classical music; candles; plenty of soft towels; the ultimate spa attire: a comfortable bath robe and slippers and anything else that would make this home experience even more heavenly. If you wish, as a treat, book a massage session with a massage therapist.

This time is just for you; inform your immediate circle that you will not be available. Disconnect from your screens and phone; resist the temptation to check messages. Once your body gets used to regular quiet spa time, you will notice that you relax more quickly and more deeply, making you feel peaceful, balanced and healthier.

Most of the following spa tools can be purchased at your local drug store: loofah brush, skin brush, cellulite massager, pumice stone, friction glove or exfoliating bath mitt, cooling eye mask, eye pillow, bath pillow, foot bath, candles, music, and mixing bowls like those from your kitchen.

What we need to feel better is often very simple and comes from Mother Nature.
All we have to do is go to her.

French Pot Pourri

This fragrant blend sets the mood to create a sensual ambiance inviting you to relax and enjoy your spa care ritual. It indicates that this is your time out to experience the 5 Rs: Relax, Reflect, Replenish, Rejuvenate and Re-create.

3 cups dried rose petals and buds
1½ cups dried peppermint leaves
1½ cups lavender
2 tbsp dried rosemary leaves
¼ vanilla bean, finely chopped
1 tsp ground cinnamon
1 cinnamon stick, broken in pieces
½ tsp ground clove
5 whole cloves
2 pieces orange zest, approximately 2 inches each

5 drops rosemary essential oil
5 drops orange essential oil
1 drop patchouli essential oil

Mix the herbs and spices in a clear decorative glass container or jar. Add the essential oils and mix well. Stir periodically to release the fragrance. Add more essential oils when needed. To retain the fragrance, cover the jar when you are not using the pot pourri.

Water

Spa: The name of a town in Belgium known for the healing properties of its water, it is often used as a Latin acronym for *salus per aquam,* meaning "health by water". The Water element consists of aspects of nurturance, cleansing and nourishment, all leading to healing and wellness.

Water is crucial to life on Earth for all living beings. It also plays a very important part in a spa environment. The surface of our planet is covered mainly by water – 70 to 75%, and so are our bodies. We are made mostly of water; we need water to live, drink, eat, cleanse inside and out, detox and revitalize. When we drink water, we facilitate the release of toxins through our pores and our eliminating system. By bathing, we cleanse ourselves from the outside in, as our bathwater penetrates our skin. Be mindful of what you put in your bathwater! Remember to drink water to rehydrate yourself during and after your bath experience.

It is through relaxation that you can find the path to healing and wellness.
Give yourself the gift of relaxation on a regular basis.

Basic Bath Salts

I see the beach and the ocean as a refreshing garden for inspiration and my favourite vacation destination. Nothing re-energizes and "resets" me better than walking in the sand and feeling the salty air on my skin. Between beach vacations, using sea salt, seaweed, sponges, conch shells, ocean waves CDs, and essential oils, I can create an "ocean bath experience" that gives me the feeling of being in the Caribbean. I sit back in the tub, relax and visualize my next vacation.

Saltwater has special cleansing and healing properties: it helps draw toxins out of the body. Saltwater is very similar to our bodily fluids and our blood plasma. In a saltwater bath, the water permeates our skin, cleans it out, and replaces the toxin-filled fluids.

2 cups salt (sea salt or kosher or Himalayan salt)
¼ cup baking soda (to soften the skin)
12-15 drops essential oil(s) of your choice

In a glass or stainless-steel bowl, mix the ingredients together. Store in a jar. At bath time, pour ½ cup of the salt mixture into the tub and add warm water. Stir the water to dissolve the salt. Enjoy!

Relaxing Bath Salts

1¼ cups sea salt
½ cup Epsom salt
¼ cup baking soda
¾ cup chamomile flowers
¼ cup calendula petals, chopped (if you can find some)

¼ cup rose petals
2 tbsp lavender buds
10 drops chamomile essential oil
15 drops lavender essential oil
A piece of cheese cloth and some string or a mesh bag

In a glass or stainless-steel bowl, mix all the ingredients together. Store in a glass jar. At bath time, place ½ cup of the salt mixture in the centre of the cheesecloth. Gather the corners to create a bundle and tie with the string. If you are using a mesh bag, pour the salt mixture in it. From the string, suspend the bundle or the mesh bag on the tub tap to let the water run through it, or let it float in the water. Get in the tub, sit back, and relax. You can do deep-breathing sequences to relax and calm the nervous system. Please refer to **Health-building Block #5** for details.

Energizing Mediterranean Bath Salts

1¼ cups sea salt
½ cup Epsom salt
¼ cup baking soda
3 tbsp rosemary leaves
1½ tbsp rose petals
2 tsp orange or lemon zest
1 tbsp lemon verbena leaves, chopped

1½ tbsp lavender buds
1½ tbsp peppermint leaves
15 drops lavender essential oil
6 drops orange essential oil
5 drops rosemary essential oils
A piece of cheese cloth and some string or a mesh bag

In a glass or stainless-steel bowl, mix all the ingredients together. Store in a glass jar. At bath time, place ½ cup of the salt mixture in the centre of the cheesecloth. Gather the corners to create a bundle and tie with the string. If you are using a mesh bag, pour the salt mixture in it. From the string, suspend the bundle or the mesh bag on the tub tap to let the water run through it, or let it float in the water. Get in the tub, sit back, and breathe deeply the energizing aromas.

French Milk Bath

Soothing and sensual, this gentle bath treat will make you feel relaxed and pampered. Add deep-breathing sequences, and you will feel renewed.

In a bowl, mix together the following ingredients. Pour into an old-fashioned milk bottle if you like. At bath time, pour the milk mixture in the warm water.

1 cup powdered milk
¼ cup Epsom salt
1 tbsp baking soda
1 tbsp cornstarch
2 tbsp ground oats
2 tbsp lavender flowers
1 tbsp dried rose petals, crushed

8 drops lavender essential oil
1 tsp or more rose water
Optional: a few drops of ylang ylang essential oil, and a few fresh rose petals to float on the water.

Consider taking a different type of bath -- a "forest bath"!
The Japanese call it shinrin-yoku. They believe that spending time in green spaces with lots of trees,
like parks and forests, helps reduce stress, strengthen the immune system and energize the body.
(In mid-December, I like to go to the garden and nursery centre and walk between the hanging Christmas trees.
The "hugging" feeling from the branches and the intoxicating coniferous aroma make me feel very happy.
My favourite fragrant soft-needle "hugger" is the white pine tree. I can't get enough of it!)

Soothing Body Scrub
(Adapted from the recipe in *Spa Magic**, by Mary Muryn)

A wonderful exfoliating scrub for sensitive, dry or itchy skin.

1 cup oatmeal
1 handful rose petals
½ cup honey
½ cup sea salt
1 tbsp warm milk
3-4 drops lavender essential oil

Roughly grind the oatmeal and the rose petals in a spice grinder. In a small bowl, blend the oatmeal, the petals, the honey, and the salt. Add the warm milk and the lavender. While you draw a warm bath with bath salts and essential oils of your choice, *gently* massage your body with the mixture using a friction bath glove or an exfoliating bath mitt. Soak in the tub for about 20 minutes allowing the mixture on your body to dissolve into the water. Rinse off well, pat dry your skin and apply a moisturizing lotion made with natural ingredients.

---

* Please refer to the References and Recommended Reading section for the reference.

Gentle French Facial Gommage

A natural concoction that will exfoliate and soothe your skin.

2-3 tbsp ground almonds	1 tbsp honey
2-3 tbsp plain yogurt	1-2 drops of lavender or tangerine essential oil

Mix well in a small bowl. With the index and middle fingers of each hand, gently rub the gommage on your skin in small circles for 1-2 minutes, avoiding the eye area. Rinse with lukewarm water and pat dry. While your skin is still moist, apply a nourishing lotion made with natural ingredients.

A Facial Massage Inspired by Traditional Chinese Medicine (TCM)

As you moisturize your face and throat, you can apply the lotion with a massage to benefit the skin, relax the body, and stimulate the blood flow and the acupressure points. Here is a ritual you might want to adopt: Sit comfortably; using your index and middle fingers, massage in small circles for 5 seconds on the following 3 acupressure points; then, repeat the first 3 steps 3 times. Finish with Step 4: the Gentle Palming.

For a demonstration, visit my website at www.olivestolychees.com

1. Between the eyebrows, at the root of the nose (*Yintang*). Pressure on this point is said to alleviate pain, dizziness, confusion and insomnia. It is said to help improve vision. Stroking this point has a very calming effect.
2. In the indentation of the temples (*Taiyang*). Pressure on these points help relax the facial muscles and ease headaches.
3. Directly below the pupils and in line with the lower borders of the nose (*Juliao*). Pressure on these points helps alleviate a headache and soothe digestive stress. It also relaxes the facial muscles.
4. Gentle Palming: Rub your hands together until they become warm. Supporting your elbows on your lap or on a table, lean your torso forward and place your forehead in your palms. Relax and gently hold for 30 seconds. Repeat the soothing palming over the following areas: your eyes, your cheeks, over your ears, your lower jaw, your throat, and your thymus-heart area.

Refreshing Thai Foot Soak for Tired Feet

Need I say more?

A- 1 cup sea salt or Epsom salts	**B-** 3-4 lemongrass sticks, cut in 2-inch pieces
¼ cup baking soda	5-6 kaffir lime leaves
10-15 drops peppermint essential oils	3-4 cardamom pods, crushed
	Small, smooth pebbles (optional)
	A pumice stone

1. Combine the **A** ingredients in a jar. Cover and shake well. In a teapot, combine the **B** ingredients. Cover with boiling water and let steep for 15-20 minutes.
2. While you are waiting, fill a large basin or foot bath with warm water. Strain the herbs (**B** ingredients) and add the liquid to the warm water. Add 1-2 tbsp of salts (**A** ingredients) to the bath. Swirl the water, make sure it is at the right temperature, and immerse your feet. Breathe deeply and relax as you soak your feet for 10 minutes. If you are using the pebbles, you can pick them up and release them with your toes for a few minutes. Make sure you stay hydrated by drinking water or herbal tea.
3. When the skin of your feet has softened, use a pumice stone and rub off the rough skin on your heels. Pat your feet dry and moisturize with a natural ingredients lotion or cream. Put on a pair of cotton socks and continue your spa care ritual.

'Farniente' is the art of doing nothing, being in a state of blissful inaction.
When was the last time you sat outside and just watched the clouds (or the people) shuffle by?

Foot and Hand Salt Scrub

It is a great scrub to exfoliate and stimulate the skin. Rub on feet, hands, elbows, and knees. Rinse off with water only. Pat dry and moisturize. Keep the unused portion in a sealed jar.

A. Dry ingredients

In a small bowl, mix together 1 tbsp Epsom salt, 1 tsp sea salt, and 1 tsp baking soda.

B. Wet ingredients

In another small bowl, mix together ½ to 1 tsp gycerin, ½ to 1 tsp coconut oil and a few drops of floral water. Add just enough to the above dry ingredients for viscosity. You can also add 1-2 drops of essential oils such as lavender, rosewood, ylang ylang, pine or petitgrain. If the consistency is a little too moist, add small amounts of salts and baking soda.

Moroccan Red Clay Cleansing Mask

Spread a thin layer of the mask over your face and allow it to penetrate the skin. Take some time to sit back, sip some tea and relax. Rinse thoroughly with lukewarm water using your fingers or a soft cloth. Pat dry and hydrate with a lotion made with natural ingredients. Refrigerate the unused portion of the mask in a closed jar in the refrigerator, and use within 2 weeks.

For oily skin, use once a week and leave the mask on your face for at least 15 minutes.
For normal to dry skin, use every other week and leave the mask on your face for 8-10 minutes.

A. Wet ingredients

Mix together in a small bowl:

½ cup lotion or cream base (I like to use Burt's Bees® Body Lotion for sensitive skin for its natural ingredients.)
3 drops each of jasmine, tangerine, and palmarosa essential oils☺
1 tsp honey

B. Dry ingredients

Add the following ingredients to the above mixture and mix well.

1½ tsp ground dried adzuki beans (you can grind the beans yourself in a spice grinder)	½ tsp green clay
½ tbsp powdered milk	1 tsp ground oatmeal (you can grind the flakes in a spice grinder)
½ tbsp Moroccan red clay	

☺If you don't have these oils, don't worry; the mask will still be effective and pleasant.

A Restful Sleep Synergy

In a spray bottle, mix distilled water, 7-8 drops of lavender essential oil, and a few drops of chamomile and marjoram essential oils. Shake to combine well. Spray in the bedroom and on the bed linen. No chamomile or marjoram? Use lavender essential oil, orange blossom water or rose water.

Your body needs plenty of rest to restore itself and heal. Good quality sleep in the right amount is vital to the overall wellbeing. Besides having a beneficial impact on the immune function, metabolism, learning, memory and other vital physiological functions, a good night's sleep provides the body with an opportunity to rest, recharge and renew. After a good night's sleep, you may notice an increase in your productivity; your physical, mental and emotional energy is more balanced and steady, and you are in a better mood. To get more quality sleep, aim to go to bed earlier than usual. If possible, have a 10 to 20-minute afternoon nap to recharge your battery. The numerous benefits of an afternoon nap are recognized by an increasing number of employers. In fact, in some Japanese companies, the afternoon nap is mandatory!

Without enough sleep, I feel like a cranky two-year old.

Twelve tips for a better night of sleep

1. *Have an early light dinner* so your sleep will not be disturbed by laborious digestion. A walk outside may help you sleep better.
2. After dinner, *relax in* a *warm bath*. Add some of the **Relaxing Bath Salts** to the water if you like. Allow yourself to relax your muscles, close your eyes, breathe deeply and calm your mind. Refer to the **Health-building Block #5** for the breathing sequence. **Steps 3** to **5** can also be done while you soak in the tub. When you drain the tub after your bath, imagine that your worries and stress are flowing away with the water.
3. *Put on some pajamas or a night gown* instead of gym clothes (a T-shirt and sweat pants). This signals to the body that the work day is over and it is time to get ready for bed to rest.
4. *Release your worries.* Before going to sleep, write down your concerns and what weighs on your mind. Add possible solutions and your desired outcome. Give yourself permission to let go: you have done what you can. Go to sleep with a clear mind. You may receive guidance during your sleep or when you wake up in the morning. Keep a notepad and a pen on your night table to record dreams and inspiration.
5. Sit comfortably and *sip a soothing herbal tea*, like chamomile, or a cup of hot water with a slice of lemon in it. *Breathe deeply*, relax your body and calm your mind.
6. *Listen to relaxing music.* Classical music, nature recordings or any recording of 60 beats per minute designed to slow down the brain waves are great choices to put you in sleep mode. Watching the news on television before bed or in bed is not conducive to restful sleep. In fact, studies show it is best to avoid using electronics a few hours before bedtime because the exposure to their artificial bright light can disturb our sleep patterns.
7. *Reading positive affirmations or inspiring books* ensures that you have an uplifting mental program before allowing your subconscious to do its nocturnal work. Unwinding with a recorded guided meditation or gentle yin yoga poses will also put you in the mood for peaceful slumber.
8. Determine how many hours you need to sleep to feel rested and refreshed in the morning. *Set a definite bed time and honour it* as you honour your other commitments. Do you need an alarm clock to wake up? With enough restful sleep, you will eventually be able to wake up on your own, which is more pleasant than being jolted by the sound of the alarm.
9. *Sleep as long as long as you need to.* Don't feel guilty about needing more sleep, especially if you are not getting enough on a regular basis. See restorative sleep as your remedy to support greater health and happiness. Whenever possible, rest when you are tired and take the time to sleep.
10. For quality sleep, *keep the bedroom temperature on the cool side* between 65 and 68°F.
11. To prevent noise disturbances coming from outside (or inside) your home, *use a fan in your bedroom to create white noise* so you stay asleep all night long.
12. Should you wake up in the middle of the night and you are unable to fall back asleep because your mind is taking you in all directions, *focus on your breathing to slow down your brain activity* and bring you -- mind, body and spirit -- back in the present time. Sweet dreams!

Your Pledge:

On _____ _____ _____, _____
　(date)'　　　　　(month)'　　　(year),　　　　　　　　　　　　　　　　　(your name)

started a **Spa Care Ritual** to nourish and nurture mind, body and spirit.

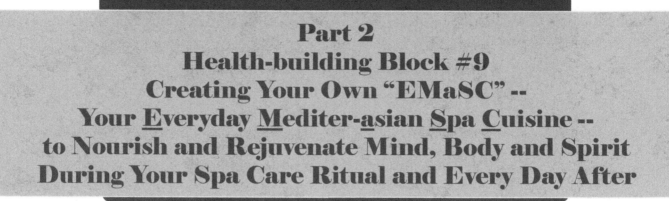

Part 2
Health-building Block #9
Creating Your Own "EMaSC" --
Your Everyday Mediter-asian Spa Cuisine --
to Nourish and Rejuvenate Mind, Body and Spirit
During Your Spa Care Ritual and Every Day After

*Take control of how you nourish and heal your body by learning to cook your own healthy meals with real ingredients,
especially if you suffer from allergies, food intolerances, and health issues.
Proper nourishment with real food is one of the wellness foundation pillars.*

Please note that none of the recipes in this book contain wheat, yeast, gluten, peanut, grain, corn, GMO soy, refined sugar. To replace the soy sauce in Asian dishes, I recommend using very small amounts of organic wheat-free Tamari sauce made with organic non-GMO soy beans. Some recipes call for full fat, organic dairy in the form of butter, cheese, cream or plain Greek yogurt. For many of these recipes, the dairy is optional.

The preparation and cooking times are approximate depending on your cooking skills, kitchen equipment and environment. You may need to add 5-10 minutes, or more, to the suggested times, especially the first time you experiment with a recipe. To avoid rushing, getting frustrated and injuring yourself, allow yourself extra time to cook.

To ensure successful cooking sessions with minimal to no aggravation at all, here is what *I strongly suggest*:

1. *Look at cooking as a fun craft project* that will give you an edible and tasty art piece at the end;
2. As you would for any recipe in other cookbooks, *read the whole recipe* you are interested in *before starting to cook;*
3. *Assemble all the required ingredients, supplies, and kitchen equipment.* If you are missing 1 or 2 ingredients and can do without or can replace them with different ones, great! You can proceed with the *mise en place* (cutting and measuring all ingredients and keeping them in prep bowls or plates, ready for a smooth cooking and assembling process. This important step in food preparation can be done several hours ahead; the prep bowls are covered with plastic wrap and kept in the refrigerator.) If you can't modify the recipe, choose another one that lists the ingredients you currently have on hand. Remember, the recipes are only guidelines. Feel free to write on sticky notes or directly in the book your own modifications for the recipes that you experiment with. The dishes you prepare will be amazing and truly nourishing when you use your creative passion and intuition, and you infuse them with your personal loving touch.
4. *Wear an apron to protect your clothes.* I have ruined enough tops to know that I need one, not because I am a messy cook, but because unexpected splashes and stains can ruin a top I like. I see my apron as the kitchen uniform that I put on when I pull out my knives, cutting board and prep bowls. My whole being, at a cellular level, knows that I am about to do some serious playing with food! It feels like something is missing when I start preparing food without wearing it, just like getting in the car or in an airplane seat and not buckling up. Also, to be able to stand comfortably for long periods of time when I am cooking up a storm, I always wear a pair of indoor shoes; otherwise I tend to get sore feet and legs.
5. *Being comfortable* in what we do and finding enjoyment in it is important as that energy of comfort and enjoyment is transferred to our work and, by extension, to the food we cook. Otherwise, no comfort or enjoyment: why bother? So, relax, be mindful of each slice of knife, of each swirl of spoon, of each sample tasting. Enjoy the process of cooking and the magic that will manifest from your loving efforts.

Most of the spa recipes that follow can be prepared in less than 30-45 minutes. Some recipes like the classic *Pot-au-feu au bœuf,* and the *Italian Minestrone* require more preparation and cooking time to develop maximum flavours and become delicious, comforting spa food. They are great weekend projects with the family's help or when you have a few free hours. They require a bit more work but the end product is so rewarding and enjoyable! You know that, once the dish is performing its magic in the pot, you are free to do other things. Just check on it once in a while and follow your nose!

Nourish. Enjoy. Flourish.

Just like for many foodies, cooking is a huge part of my life. My kitchen is where I celebrate happy moments and where I find comforting nourishment during the challenging times. In those times, when my vision gets blurry and tears begin to sprinkle the food, I stop, acknowledge what is going on, and resume the food preparation.

Cooking grounds me; it helps me find my centre again. Like gardening, it is an activity that I can get lost in and come out with a renewed sense of balance, a feeling of accomplishment ... and a delicious dish to share.

A great cookbook for me is an invitation to converse and explore; it is also igniting the desire to make some of the recipes, if not all of them! To my great delight, many cookbooks – and cooking shows – are fulfilling that invitation rather than making cooking an intimidating performance.

Cooking is about enjoying my time in the kitchen guided by intuition and senses. It is about being in the moment, sharing and savouring the nourishment that allows me to thrive and flourish. According to the <u>Gage Canadian Dictionary</u>, the definition of *flourish* is *"the state of being in the best time of life"*. In challenging times, it is important to be mindful of the quality of our nourishment so we can continue to thrive and flourish.

Mindfulness and Clean Eating

Just like the first volume on the Art and the Pleasure of Eating Well, this volume of the <u>*Everyday Mediter-asian Spa Cuisine*</u> Collection is a *nourishment plan focusing on endless possibilities rather than restrictions*. The following easy recipes will help you create dishes with great eye appeal that will make your guests wonder how much time you spent cooking. The "clean" dishes are filled with nourishing properties that will make everyone feel and look good.

Spa food doesn't have to be "blah" food. Spa food is tasty and satisfying. Spa Food is *clean eating*. As I mentioned in Volume 1, *"Clean eating" is about being open-minded and mindful. Being open-minded* is about being willing to make beneficial life changes, and to experiment with new foods, new ways of cooking and eating. *Being mindful* is about making better choices when shopping for ingredients, selecting snacks and dishes when eating at home or out. By slowing down to eat, you are better able to savour your food, and your brain has time to signal to your stomach that it is becoming full.

Clean eating is one of many ways of addressing health and wellness issues. It is about raising your energy and vibration, boosting your immunity, reducing inflammation in the body, and maintaining optimal health to live a vibrant life. *Being aware* of the food you are eating and knowing why it is so essential for the wellness of your mind, body and spirit enables you to realize your cleansing and healing goals. *Clean eating* means that you are in charge of what you eat: taking the time to prepare your own meals with a variety of real, organic (whenever possible) ingredients -- fresh produce, meats, nuts and seeds, oils. It means avoiding processed and packaged foods, refined sugar, GMOs, additives, food colourings, etc. It also means *noticing* how you feel after eating certain foods, i.e., satisfied, energized, happy: great! Lethargic, bloated, gassy, unwell: avoid these foods as they do not agree with you! We are all different and have unique wellness needs. Not all healthy foods are good for everyone on a regular basis. For example, we are encouraged to eat "an apple a day to keep the doctor away". Not everyone can digest an apple. You are the authority on your health.

Being a mindful eater is about becoming aware of the connection between your food choices and how you feel on a regular basis. Here are a few examples of popular food choices:

- <u>Breakfast</u>: toasts, croissants, bagels, pastry, sweet caffeinated beverage
- <u>Lunch</u>: pasta, sandwich, sweet beverage
- <u>Snack</u>: sweet treat, sweet caffeinated beverage
- <u>Dinner</u>: pasta, alcohol, dessert

The possible effects of these food choices:

- Excess body weight
- Persistent exhaustion
- Disturbed sleep
- IBS
- Bloating, gas

- Acne or skin blemishes
- Frequent colds and infections
- Mood swings
- Carbs and sweets cravings, etc.

You probably have heard that food is medicine. An ideal "nourishment plan" is nourishing, protecting, healing, and energizing for the body for the long term, unlike a temporary diet. Therefore, it is important, when planning your meals, to choose the right building blocks that your body needs and, for your eating enjoyment, to flavour your dishes with various ingredients from around the world. By keeping the dishes simple, tasty and enjoyable, you will soon forget about your old eating habits. You will feel more energized with a spring in your step, a sparkle in your eyes and a healthful glow on your cheeks.

I know how challenging it can be to change any habit, and breaking dietary habits is even more challenging. Because we are so attached to our food preferences, our taste buds rule us. I know, I have made many changes in my nourishment plan over the years, and I am still "grieving" the foods I miss. However, envisioning the big picture and my future, I have made the choice to invest in my health and raise my vibration with the best building blocks. As I have experienced, you, too, will notice that once you start feeling better, energized and symptom-free, you will want to initiate more changes in your nourishment plan *and* lifestyle. I bet you will be surprised at how easy it is to make the necessary changes to feel better, healthier and more productive. You will wonder why you didn't start this journey to greater health sooner.

The important thing to keep in mind is to become aware of *how you feel* before and after eating, notice what food(s) make you feel ill, and be mindful of that when choosing, cooking and eating your food. Your body is very wise; it is constantly trying to keep you well and in balance, despite your habits and transgressions. Your food choices can make you sick and cause serious illnesses; or they can heal and even prevent illnesses. You are the authority regarding your body and your health. Value your health, your potential and your life. That is where your energies and focus should be directed to.

There are as many ideal nourishment plans as there are individuals. Take the time to experiment which one works best for you at this time in your life. My ideal nourishment plan is one that provides me with focused and steady energy, a good night's sleep, and a body that is free of pain during the day and at night. It is a plan that makes me feel great and happy, able to focus on other things than low energy and pain management. I am not perfect; I aim at being as consistent as possible, and avoid temptation! And when I deviate from my *clean* food path for some reasons (usually when I travel), I enjoy my food selection and, when I return home, I get back to preparing my own produce-filled meals.

What Would Your Ideal Nourishment Plan Do For You?

There is no point in making radical changes in your eating patterns. To ensure your happiness and success, it might be wise that you *ease* into your healthier nourishment plan by adopting *ONE* positive change at a time. This way, the transition is more easily bridged and less daunting. By focusing on *ONE* change or new habit at a time, and experimenting how it works for you, you have a greater chance of successfully maintaining the new habit and build other healthy ones on it.

What worked for me was to avoid just *one* food item (gluten) and concentrate on adding more of what I needed in my meals -- water, fiber, vegetables, protein, nuts, oils, exciting flavours – instead of focusing on what I couldn't eat. When preparing meals, I concentrated on the endless possibilities rather than the few restrictions. The new frequencies that I was introducing into my body were resonating with me and my higher aspirations for greater wellness. I saw my new food choices as building blocks and fuel for success.

For you, it could be about avoiding sugar and sweet treats, or fast food meals, or dairy, or convenience-packaged food, or take-out meals, or anything you feel ready to let go of. Trust that you can do it and start your new journey to wellness.

Next, as I started to feel better (clearer head, increased overall energy, better sleep, decreasing body pain, steady happy moods, flatter stomach, feeling lighter in my body, reduced carbs cravings), it was easier to avoid another problematic food for me: dairy. Without dairy, my skin cleared up and so did my throat and my sinuses. Because dairy and wheat are mucous-forming, I felt the constant need to clear my throat and nose. Also, the excess weight started to come off, gradually, as I focused on the building blocks of health -- *quality meats, fresh produce, nuts and seeds, and oils*. (It became the guiding motto that I still repeat to myself when planning meals.) My taste buds were no longer craving the gluten products, the dairy and the sugar. With plenty of fresh produce, nuts and seeds, oils and meats to choose from, it is fun to create exciting and satisfying dishes, three meals a day.

The kitchen is where transformation (and magic!) happens. When you cook healthy meals with fresh, high-energy plant food, you have the power to transform your health and that of your loved ones, as well as your lives. When your nourishment plan is based on a variety of real, fresh ingredients that you cook yourself, you don't need to fuss about calorie count, and having to over-exert yourself to burn excess calories because you feel bloated and guilty. Remember, *real food* is life-giving and a source of enjoyment.

I look forward to joining you in your kitchen, through this nourishment-for-wellness book open on your counter, guiding you through the tasty nourishing meal ideas that follow. I know you will be pleased with your spa dishes made with the natural essences of real, honest ingredients, and so will the people you cook for.

I invite you to put on your apron – how about getting a new one to mark the beginning of this journey to greater health? -- pull out your cutting board and knife, and let's get cooking!

Here is my **Nourishment Therapy Formula** for a healthy and happy life:

Honest De-cluttering

+ Wise Shopping

+ Intuitive Cooking

+ Mindful Eating

+ Regular Home Spa Rejuvenating

———————————————————————

Vibrant Living!

To experience happiness and vitality,
cook your own delicious meals with fresh plant food full of prana (life force energy).

Breakfast

The most important meal of the day as it "breaks the fast".
It can be nutritious, quick and easy to prepare;
or a more elaborate, sit-down, no-hurry meal to splurge with the family on the weekend.
One thing is for sure, we should start the day with **real food,** not refined or processed;
something delicious and nourishing that will fuel us mentally and physically to face the day ahead.

Throughout the day, make water your beverage of choice for hydration and to maintain high energy level.
Coffee has a dehydrating effect and, once the caffeine effect has worn off,
it leaves you feeling flat, tired and craving for another "lift".
Following are a few breakfast ideas that are designed to provide steady energy
and don't include the common ingredients that cause intolerance in many people: grains, gluten, refined sugar.
If you suspect that dairy and eggs are causing you digestive discomfort
or are making you feel tired after a meal, it is best that you avoid them.
In the recipes calling for cheese or yogurt, you can omit these ingredients,
and the recipes will still be delicious.
If you have an intolerance to eggs, you may want to experiment with vegetable recipes for breakfast
with some form of protein like nuts and seeds, chicken, or fish,
a breakfast menu that is not unusual in countries like China and Japan.
For breakfast, after some fruits, I often have a vegetable soup and/or a salad or steamed vegetables with some
nuts or a few bites of cooked meat. It sustains me until lunch; I don't feel the need to reach for a snack.
It is possible to re-think your breakfast options by choosing anything healthy and non-sugary.
Trust that breakfast doesn't have to be bread, cereals or eggs and bacon!
Fire up your imagination with the recipe ideas from this book and Volume 1
and write down your new creations.
I hope that the following recipes will inspire you to make breakfast and take the time to enjoy it,
preferably sitting down, wherever you take it.

Get-Out-of-Bed Broiled Grapefruit

Serves 4
Prep Time: 15 min.
Cooking Time: 5 min.

When the fragrance of the warm spices will be floating throughout your house, everyone will be getting out of bed and rushing to the breakfast table. It is a great "Intro to Breakfast Treat" when you are not quite hungry yet for a full spread.

1-2 tbsp cane or coconut sugar
¼ tsp ground ginger
⅛ tsp ground nutmeg
¼ tsp each ground cinnamon and ground clove
2 tbsp softened butter

2 large grapefruit, at room temperature,
cut in half crosswise

1. In a small bowl, combine the sugar, all the spices and the softened butter together. Set aside.
2. Position the broiler rack several inches away from the heating element. Preheat the broiler.

3. With a curved grapefruit knife or a regular sharp knife, section each grapefruit half by cutting between the rind and the pulp, and on either sides of each dividing membrane, so each grapefruit segment can be easily spooned out at serving time.
4. Smear the sweet spicy butter mixture on the cut side of every grapefruit half. Transfer the grapefruit halves to the broiler pan or a baking dish. Broil until the topping is bubbly and lightly browned, about 5 minutes. Transfer to serving dishes and serve while hot.

Cin-almond Pancakes

Makes 6-8
Prep Time: 10 min.
Cooking Time: 10 min.

This healthy high-fiber, high-protein breakfast is a refreshing option from the regular high-carb version. Whether or not you are a morning person, you will agree that a delicious breakfast starts the day off on a high note.

2 eggs	1 tbsp melted coconut oil
¾ cup almond milk	¼ cup unsweetened apple juice
2 tbsp coconut flour	1 tbsp cinnamon
3 tbsp hemp seeds	Pinch of Celtic salt
2 tbsp flaxseeds	

1. In a blender, combine all ingredients until smooth. Pour the batter in a measuring cup and let it rest for a few minutes while you warm up some butter or coconut oil in a pan or skillet.
2. For each pancake, pour about 1-2 tbsp of batter in the hot non-stick pan or skillet. Cook over medium-low heat for about 3 minutes; then, flip the pancake to the other side and cook for another minute.

Variations:

- Add fresh berries: like blueberries or raspberries after the batter is combined in the blender.
- Make your own quick syrup: In a small saucepan, combine ½ cup **orange juice**, 2 tbsp of your favorite **jam** (I like the jam from *Bonne Maman* for its simple real ingredients) and ½ tsp ground **cinnamon and/or cloves**. Heat and stir until the jam has melted and spices are incorporated. Pour over the warm pancakes.
- Make a warm compote: In a small saucepan, combine 1 cup of chopped **apples**, 1 tsp (or more) ground **cinnamon**, 1 tsp ground **cloves**, 1 chopped round of **candied ginger**, 1 tbsp **butter or coconut oil**, 2 tbsp **unsweetened apple juice**. Cook for several minutes until the apples are soft and fragrant.

Create-Your-Own Frittata

Serves 4-6
Prep Time: 20 min.
Cooking Time: 15 min.

Like an omelet, this dish can be served for breakfast, or a light lunch with a salad. You can add any filling you like. It is a great way to use extra ingredients from a previous recipe or the leftovers of a previous meal such as:

- chopped vegetables (cooked mushrooms, cooked potatoes, fresh or roasted red pepper, zucchini, leeks, pitted olives)
- small cubes or strips of cooked meats (turkey, ham, bacon, smoked salmon, shrimp)
- grated cheese or a combination of cheeses (chèvre, boursin, bocconcini, emmenthal, swiss, parmesan, cheddar, feta, etc.)
- freshly chopped herbs (parsley, basil, oregano, chives, thyme, dill, coriander, mint, etc.)

7-8 eggs	¼ cup water

Celtic salt and pepper to taste
2 tbsp butter or coconut oil
½ cup onion or less, chopped
1 garlic clove, minced
½ cup of the vegetables of your choice

1 cup of the meat of your choice
Optional toppings: ¾ cup of the cheese of your choice
¼ cup chopped herb or
1 tbsp of the **Nourishing Japanese Sprinkle Mix**
from the **Extra Nourishment** section.

1. In a medium bowl, whisk the eggs, water, salt and pepper. Set aside.
2. In a 9-10" non-stick, oven-proof pan, melt the butter over medium heat. Swirl the pan so the melted butter coats the bottom and the sides of the pan.
3. Add the onion. Cook for 5 minutes, until translucent, over medium heat.
4. Add the garlic and the vegetables and cook for a few minutes.
5. Pour the egg mixture over the vegetable mixture. Sprinkle the meat cubes, grated cheese and herbs. Cook over medium-low heat for about 5-7 minutes or until the bottom and the sides of the frittata have firmed up and the top is still undercooked.
6. In the mean-time, preheat the broiler.
7. Put the pan under the broiler and cook for about 2 minutes, or until the frittata is set and golden. Remove from oven and let cool for a few minutes before serving.

Grain-free Granola

Makes 3-4 cups
Prep Time: 5-10 min.
Cooking Time: 15-20 min.

Here is a healthier version than the store-bought kind. It contains little sugar and is great with fresh berries or stone fruits. You can also use it as a topping for natural yogurt, spiced applesauce or an apple crisp. You can find the **Spiced Applesauce** recipe in the **Breakfast** section of **Volume 1**. This mix can also be used as a breakfast cereal.

2 cups almonds, roughly chopped
¼ cup of raisins, roughly chopped
¼ cup dried fruits such as apricots, cherries, apples, pears, goji berries, roughly chopped
¼ cup dried unsweetened coconut flakes
¾ cup sunflower seeds
¼ cup each of whole flaxseeds and ground flaxseeds

¼ cup each of hemp seeds and chia seeds
¼ cup maple syrup
1 tsp vanilla
1 tsp cinnamon
½ tsp each of ground cloves and ginger
½ tsp Celtic salt

1. Preheat oven to 350°F. Put all ingredients in a mixing bowl. Using a spatula, combine well.
2. Line a baking sheet with parchment paper. Spread the mixture over the baking sheet. Bake for 15-20 minutes, or until golden, fragrant and dried.
3. Let cool. Store in a glass container in the refrigerator or in the freezer. It can keep for 3-4 weeks refrigerated, and 2 months frozen.

Nectarine and Blueberry Yogurt

Serves 2
Prep Time: 10 min.

This simple breakfast idea can be a mid-morning or mid-afternoon snack.
For a dairy-free version, it is very enjoyable without the yogurt.

2 nectarines or peaches, stones
removed and cut into chunks
1 cup fresh blueberries
1½ cups Greek natural yogurt
1 tsp honey or maple syrup, if desired

2 tbsp ground flaxseeds
¼ tsp ground nutmeg
1 tbsp flaxseed oil
¼ cup almonds or hazelnuts, whole or chopped

Divide the fruits in 2 bowls.
Top with yogurt, sweetener (if using), flaxseeds, nutmeg, and flaxseed oil. Mix together.
Scatter the nuts on top.

I cannot accept anymore emergencies, I am already booked solid!

Œufs en cocottes
(Baked eggs)

Serves 4
Prep Time: 10-15 min.
Cooking Time: 15-20 min.

If you are looking for a new way to serve eggs for a weekend breakfast, try these baked eggs.
You can also turn this easy and quick breakfast idea into a lunch menu item to accompany a green salad
and/or a side dish of steamed vegetables.

4 ramekins, buttered or oiled
1-2 boiled potatoes, cut in ¼-inch slices
½ cup Boursin cheese
⅓ cup sun-dried tomatoes, chopped
or small cubes of cooked ham

A small handful of shredded spinach or arugula leaves
Chopped herbs such as chives, parsley, basil
4 eggs
Black pepper and hot pepper flakes
¼ cup grated parmesan or 1 tbsp ground flaxseeds

1. Preheat oven to 375°F.
2. Cover the bottom of each ramekin with 1-2 potato slices, depending on their size.
3. Divide the Boursin in 4 portions and place one portion on top of the potato slices.
4. Divide the sun-dried tomatoes in each ramekin, as well as the spinach or arugula, and the herbs.
5. Crack an egg over the tomato-herb mixture in each of the ramekin. Season with pepper and hot pepper flakes. Sprinkle with parmesan or flaxseeds.
6. To carry the ramekins more easily to the oven, place them in a baking dish. Bake for 15-20 minutes, or until the eggs are cooked to your liking. Serve the hot ramekins on small plates.

While Waiting for the Next Meal

Snacks and Beverages

The following healthy spa beverages can be enjoyed as a snack during a rest period or between meals. They are simple and quick to prepare. Feel free to add other produce, herbs, spices and superfoods that you may have on hand for added taste and nourishment. Some recipes do not show an exact quantity of ingredients because I use a little bit of this, a handful of that to fit the blender and suit my palate. Before pouring the blend in a nice glass, I taste and decide if I need to add anything else.

If the batch you make yields more than you can enjoy at the time, pour the extra portion in a thermos (or a container with a tight lid) and keep it in the refrigerator for later. Some of these beverages may oxidize and change colour. As for any freshly made drinks, it is best to consume these beverages immediately for optimum taste, visual appeal and nutritional benefits. I use a blender or a Vitamix® (a high-speed blender). The recipes make 1-2 servings.

Every time I hear the word 'diet', I want chocolate!

Frappé au concombre et à la menthe (Cucum-mint Refresher)

Two classic Mediterranean ingredients that go so well together.

1 large English cucumber, peeled
1 handful of fresh mint leaves
1 tsp honey, if desired

1 mint leaf to garnish
Some water to dilute

Cut the cucumber in half, scrape the seeds out with a spoon, and cut into chunks. Place the chunks in a blender with the mint leaves and the honey. Purée until smooth. Add a little water to thin the consistency, if necessary. Pour into a nice glass and garnish with the mint leaf.

Vietnamese Pineapple Digestive

A delicious combo that facilitates digestion. Purée all ingredients in a blender until smooth. Taste and dilute with a bit of water if you find it too sweet. Serve in a nice glass.

½ pineapple, peeled, cored and cut into chunks
Zest of ½ lime

Juice of 1 lime
4-5 fresh mint leaves

Blueberry and Peach Shake

In place of ice cubes, which I find too cold in a shake or a smoothie, I freeze in re-sealable plastic bags a few ripe bananas that I peel and cut in half. I add one half at a time with the rest of the ingredients in a blender, and purée until smooth, adding water as needed.

1-2 peaches or nectarines, pitted and quartered
1 cup fresh blueberries
1 small frozen banana, cut in chunks

½ tsp grated nutmeg
1 small round of candied ginger
Water to dilute

Fruit Sorbet or Healthy Frozen Lollipops

In a blender, purée 1 mango or 3 fresh peaches with 1 cup of orange juice and 1 tsp lime zest. For a sorbet, pour the mixture in a shallow container and freeze for a few hours, stirring with a fork whenever you think of it. To serve, take the container out of the freezer, allow to soften for 5-10 minutes, and spoon a portion of the mixture in a pretty glass. <u>For frozen lollipops</u>, pour the fruit mixture into an ice cube tray and plant toothpicks in each compartment. Cover with a plastic wrap and freeze. Enjoy this refreshing treat. You can also experiment with other fruits, a little fruit juice or water, some zest and you have a new frozen delight. It makes a great spa dessert, too!

Merveille de santé verte (Healthy Green Wonder)

To keep this beverage interesting, you can vary the greens by adding or substituting some cucumber chunks and a handful of fresh parsley. Put all ingredients in a high-power blender and blend until smooth.
If you want extra "wonder", add a good pinch of ground turmeric.

4 romaine lettuce leaves	½ Granny Smith apple
A small handful of spinach leaves	1 tsp chlorella or spirulina
1 kale leaf	⅛ lime
1 celery rib	Water as needed
1 handful of blueberries	

Green and Orange Power

Blend the following ingredients until smooth.

A handful of kale or spinach leaves	A few chunks of pineapple
1 carrot, peeled, cut in small pieces	A pinch of turmeric
½ orange, cut in pieces	½ tsp spirulina (optional)
Orange zest	

Tisane digestive

Great to promote healthy digestion after meals.
Rinse a large teapot with hot water. Place all ingredients in a teapot. Pour hot water over them.
Cover and infuse for 15 minutes or more. Strain and discard the herbs. Sweeten if desired.
Makes about 2-4 cups.

1 tbsp dried peppermint leaves	½ tsp grated ginger with its juice
1 tbsp dried chamomile flowers	1 cinnamon stick of about 2 inches long
½ tsp fennel seeds	Honey to taste
1 tsp orange peel, chopped in small pieces	

Exotic and Comforting Tisane

This blend of exotic flavours is a delicious treat after a meal or in the afternoon. Rinse a large teapot with hot water. In the teapot, place 3-4 **kaffir lime leaves**, 1 **cinnamon stick**, 2 **star anise**, 1-2 **pieces of orange peel**, 1 **piece of candied ginger**, 1 tsp **orange blossom water**, ¼ tsp **vanilla powder** or ½ tsp **vanilla extract**, and 1 tsp **honey**, if desired. Pour hot water over the ingredients and allow to steep for a few minutes before serving.

Spanish Gazpacho

This Spanish national dish can be enjoyed as a cold soup or blended thoroughly for a refreshing beverage.
All ingredients, except the garnish, are roughly chopped before being puréed in batches in the blender until smooth.
Garnish and serve cold. Makes 2-3 servings.

⅛ small Vidalia onion (a sweet onion),
¼ English cucumber, peeled and seeded
¼ green pepper
¼ red pepper
1 small garlic clove
1 celery rib
3-4 tomatoes
A few chunks of watermelon
1 tbsp orange zest
Juice of ½ orange

1 small can of tomato juice
Celtic salt and pepper
A total of ½ cup of fresh herbs:
coriander, parsley, basil, chives
1 tbsp each of extra-virgin olive oil and balsamic vinegar
A squirt of Tabasco sauce
A pinch of Celtic salt
Garnish: 1 chopped celery rib, a few chopped
leaves of the herbs mentioned above

Indian Chai

This is a lovely Indian tea made with warm spices; you can make it as spicy or as gentle as you like.
It is a perfect drink to warm you up on a cold and damp day. There are many versions and methods to make it.
This is my favorite blend: a simple, tasty, and comforting treat. It makes 3 cups.

A- 2 cups water
2 tsp black tea leaves
4-5 whole cloves
4-5 cardamom pods
1 cinnamon stick, broken in pieces
1 star anise

¼ tsp ground ginger
⅛ tsp ground nutmeg
⅛ tsp freshly ground black pepper
1 strip or small peel of orange rind

B- 1 cup of milk (coconut, almond or cow's)
2 tbsp honey or maple syrup, to taste

1. In a saucepan, put water and tea leaves, and bring to a boil. In the meantime, with a mortar and pestle or a spice grinder, crush or grind together the whole spices. Add all the spices and the orange peel to the saucepan.
2. Let the mixture simmer for at least 5 minutes. Add milk and honey or maple syrup, and heat to near boil.
3. Remove from the heat. Strain and serve hot. Enjoy!

Thai Lemongrass and Lychees Tisane

1-2 lemongrass sticks, cut in 2-inch pieces
2-3 fresh lychees, peeled and seeded, or from a can with some of the syrup
Honey to taste if you are using fresh lychees

1. In a saucepan, boil 4 cups of water with the lemongrass pieces until fragrant.
2. Add the lychees and a few tablespoons of the reserved syrup for sweetness, if desired. Enjoy hot or chilled.

Nutritious Infused Water

Many nutritionists recommend that we drink our body weight, divided by 2, in ounces.
For example, if you weigh 150 pounds, the suggested amount of water to drink per day is: 150 ÷ 2 = 75 ounces.
It may seem a lot of water at first but it is very feasible. Here is how you can begin if you are not a water drinker yet: Start your day with a glass of warm water to get things moving and toxins flushed out of your system.
Continue drinking water throughout the day to ensure sufficient hydration for optimal energy and brain function.

Refreshing and low in calories, the following herbal-fruit ideas will transform plain water into more interesting, thirst-quenching beverages. All you have to do is fill a jug or glass bottle with good quality water and add your favourite flavour combination from the suggestions below. Allow the flavours to infuse in the refrigerator or on the counter for up to 12 hours. No excuse not to drink enough water now!

- Slices of fresh mango and lime wedges
- Slices or wedges of lime and fresh mint leaves
- Lemon slices, ½ tsp grated ginger and fresh mint leaves
- Orange slices, strawberries and fresh mint leaves
- Peach or nectarine slices, raspberries and fresh basil leaves

- Watermelon slices or cubes, cucumber slices and fresh mint leaves
- Blueberries, raspberries, blackberries and strawberries
- Frozen fruits like grapes and raspberries with fresh mint leaves
- Frozen grapes, ¼ tsp grated ginger and lime wedges

Heated **Vegetable Stock, Chicken Stock** (from **Volume 1**) and **Beef Bone Broth** are great beverages to sip before or between meals when you feel a little hungry. They are satisfying and full of goodness nourishment.

Whetting the Appetite

Appetizers

I could easily live on appetizers and **small** plates alone! Especially those containing olives!
I think serving appetizers and small plates is a unique and exciting way to eat and entertain.
The "small plate" style of eating is quite common in many European and Asian menus
where an assortment of small portions expressing a harmony of flavours is featured.
These dishes often display all the great themes of the given country's lifestyle:
simplicity, elegance, fresh ingredients, attention to detail, and a delight in miniatures.

The French are proud of their *hors d'œuvre* and *canapés,*
the Italians rave about their *antipasti,*
the Chinese love their *dim sum,*
the Spanish brag about their *tapas,*
while Greece and many Middle Eastern countries boast their *mezze.*
All with good reasons! And, I love them all!

Entertaining friends and family at home doesn't always have to be a three-course dinner party.
In fact, serving appetizers on small plates is a fresh and relaxing way to entertain, spa-style!
Organizing a casual gathering where you offer a variety of easy-to-prepare, attractive and palate-tempting
finger food is a lot of fun and allows you to fire your imagination and be as creative as you want.
As you prepare them, the appetizers can be enjoyed outside on the patio,
at the coffee table, standing up while chatting,
or simply while relaxing on a weekend afternoon.
So, pull out of your cupboards and closets the lovely small plates and dishes you forgot you had,
whether they were passed down from your grandmother or you found them at a fire sale.
Plan a delectable and healthy menu of small plates. Invite a couple of your favourite friends.
Fill the small dishes with attractive, toothsome appetizers and let the conversations get lively.
With your culinary creations and your guests singing you praises,
you will have an exciting spa-like dining experience to remember
where everyone is satisfied without over-indulging.

Spanish Marinated Olives

Serves 6-8
Prep Time: 15 min.
Marinating Time: 1 day or overnight

A very colourful appetizer that will wow your
guests. You can include small and larger olives.

Day 1:

2 cups mixed black and green olives
2 tbsp olive oil
1 tbsp lemon juice
1 unwaxed orange, scrubbed,
unpeeled, cut into small chunks
2 sprigs of rosemary
1 tsp hot pepper flakes

In a large bowl, put the olives, olive oil, lemon juice, orange pieces, rosemary, and pepper flakes. Stir gently. Cover the bowl with plastic wrap. Refrigerate for 1 day or overnight, stirring occasionally when you think about it!

Day 2:

1 small red pepper, seeded and cut into small chunks	2 dozen cherry tomatoes, quartered
1 small yellow pepper, seeded and cut into small chunks	Fresh parsley sprig for garnishing

One hour before serving, transfer the mixture to a serving bowl. Add the red pepper chunks and cherry tomatoes. Stir well, and allow to warm up to room temperature. Remove the sprigs of rosemary and replace them with fresh ones. Garnish with parsley. Provide your guests with tooth picks or little forks, and a bowl to collect the pits.

Spanish Avocado Spread

Makes 1½ cups
Prep Time: 10 min.
Refrigeration Time: 30 min.

This mixture can be used as a spread or a dip for crackers, raw vegetables like cucumber rounds, celery sticks, etc. It can also be served as an accompaniment for grilled shrimp and chicken.

1-2 garlic cloves, peeled and minced
3 avocados peeled, stoned, cut in chunks
Zest of a lime
1-2 tbsp lime juice
2 tbsp olive oil
1 tbsp fresh coriander and/or parsley, chopped
½ tsp ground cumin
Pinch of Celtic salt

Ground black pepper or hot pepper flakes
Optional: finely chopped chives for a mild onion flavour, and hot pepper flakes or harissa (¼ tsp) for a spicy version.

In a bowl, combine all ingredients and mash until smooth and creamy. Adjust the seasoning, if needed. Serve right away, or refrigerate in an airtight container for ½ hour, the surface covered with a piece of plastic wrap. Stir occasionally.

Moroccan Stuffed Dates

Serves 4
Prep Time: 10 minutes

These easy-to-make appetizers make a great snack, too.
The warm cinnamon flavour and the bright green pistachios offer great eye and palate appeal.

8 medjool dates	⅛ tsp ground cardamom
½ cup shelled, unsalted pistachios	¼ tsp Celtic salt
½ tsp ground cinnamon	1 tsp white sesame seeds

1. Slice the dates down the centre without cutting through completely. Remove the seeds. Arrange on a serving plate.
2. In a food processor, blend pistachios with cinnamon, cardamom and salt just until a sticky paste forms.
3. Spoon the pistachio paste into the dates. Sprinkle with sesame seeds and serve. Refrigerate the leftover pistachio paste for another use.

Variation:

Slice the dates down the centre without cutting through completely. Remove the seeds. Arrange on a serving plate. Stuff each date with 1 tsp of Boursin cheese. Top with a toasted almond.

Szechuan Sesame Salmon Skewers
(or the Four 'S'; try saying that 3 times!)

Makes 15-20 small skewers
Prep Time: 25 min.
Cooking Time: 5-8 min.
Chilling Time: 1 to 4 hours

These savory skewers can be made with strips of chicken, beef, and even shrimp. They are even tastier when served with the following **Orange Dipping Sauce** or **Peach and Pepper Sauce** recipes.

A- Marinade:

Combine all ingredients together in a bowl. Set aside.

1 tbsp vegetable oil	¼ tsp ground black pepper
½ tsp Chinese five-spice	1 tsp chives, finely cut with scissors
1 tsp sesame oil	1-4 tbsp each of fresh mint and coriander leaves, chopped
1 tsp organic tamari	1 tbsp toasted sesame seeds

B- 1½ lb skinless salmon fillets
15-20 wooden skewers of 6", soaked in water for 10-15 minutes before assembling to prevent scorching

1. Cut the salmon fillets crosswise, in 15-20 strips of 1" x 3". Place in a glass or ceramic dish.
2. Pour the **marinade** over the salmon strips, toss to coat. Refrigerate at least 1 hour and up to 4 hours.
3. Preheat oven to 375°F. Thread one salmon strip on a skewer. Repeat until all the strips have been skewered.
4. Place the salmon skewers in a single layer on a baking sheet. If you still have some marinade left, you can drizzle the rest over the strips. Bake for 5-8 minutes, or until cooked through but still juicy.

Orange Dipping Sauce

In a screw-top glass jar, combine the following ingredients. Screw the lid on and shake vigorously. Refrigerate until serving time.

3-4 tbsp honey	½ tsp sesame oil
3-4 tbsp rice wine vinegar	Zest of an orange
3-4 tbsp organic tamari	3-4 tbsp each of coriander and mint, chopped
1 tsp gingerroot, grated	1 tbsp toasted sesame seeds
½ tsp Sambal Oelek	

Peach and Pepper Sauce

In a medium bowl, combine all ingredients. Toss gently and refrigerate until serving time.

1 firm peach or nectarine, finely chopped	1 tsp each of lime zest and juice
1 tbsp olive oil	2 tbsp chives, finely cut with scissors
1 tbsp each of mint and basil leaves, finely chopped	½ red pepper and ½ orange pepper, finely chopped
1 small garlic clove, minced	1 tbsp rice wine vinegar
¼ tsp Sambal Oelek	½ tsp Celtic salt

Spanish Bundles

Makes 18 bundles
Prep Time: 20 min.
Cooking Time: 20 min.

These simple tapas combine the real taste and culinary spirit of Spain.

2-3 large red peppers, roasted, cooled,
carefully peeled and seeded. Set aside.
1 tsp each of finely chopped parsley and oregano
½ + ¼ tsp of fennel seeds
¼ tsp or more of hot pepper flakes
18 anchovy fillets in oil

18 green olives, pitted
1 tbsp olive oil (you can also use
some of the anchovy oil)
½ cup manchego cheese, grated (optional,
or use grated Parmesan instead)
18 long tooth picks or short skewers

1. In a small bowl, combine parsley, oregano, fennel seeds and pepper flakes. Stir to mix. Set aside.
2. Preheat oven to 425°F.
3. Cut each pepper in 6 long strips. On each strip of pepper, place 1 anchovy fillet and 1 olive. Sprinkle a pinch of the herb-spice mixture over the olive and anchovy. Wrap and roll each bundle. Thread each bundle on a tooth pick or skewer and place on a baking sheet.
4. Drizzle over some oil, sprinkle the rest of the herb-spice mixture and the grated manchego, if using.
5. Bake in hot oven for 5 minutes or until the cheese is melted and golden. Allow to cool a little before serving.

Stay in tune with your body by periodically checking in:
feel and listen for what it needs: is it nourishment, hydration, rest, movement, fresh air, a loving touch?

Vietnamese Rolls

Makes 6
Prep Time: 40-50 min.

These rolls are worth taking the time to make: they are delicious and nutritious. They are so filling and satisfying that you can even serve them as a meal with perhaps a soup and a dessert! They will be a big hit with the kids, big and small. Instead of cooked shrimp, you can use crab meat or pieces of grilled chicken.

Note: Instead of the traditional rice paper to wrap the filling, I often use large, soft salad leaves like Boston Bibb or red lettuce. If you can eat rice without any issue, use rice papers to wrap the rolls.

Spreadable Sauce:

2 tbsp of almond butter
1 tbsp or less of maple syrup
1 tsp Sambal Oelek, or to taste
1 garlic clove, grated
1 tsp gingerroot, grated
1 tsp each of rice vinegar and sesame seed oil

1 tbsp each of freshly chopped coriander and basil
Zest of 1 lime
1 tbsp lime juice
1 tsp fish sauce
1-2 tsp organic tamari
1-2 tbsp water if needed to thin the paste a little

Combine the following ingredients in a bowl until well incorporated. Taste and adjust the flavours to your palate. I tend to create this sauce, which is more like a spreadable paste, without measuring accurately: a little of this, a little of that, and taste along the way. You can make it as thick as you want it. Cover and refrigerate until serving time. You may find that this spreadable sauce tastes even better the next day!

Lettuce Rolls:

12 large soft lettuce leaves (or more,
in case you damage a few!)
1 lb shrimp, shelled, deveined,
cooked and sliced lengthwise
1-2 carrot, peeled and julienned
1 beet, peeled and julienned
1 English cucumber, julienned

½ red pepper, cut in thin strips
½ yellow pepper, cut in thin strips
½ cup snow pea shoots, or snow peas, julienned
Any other julienned vegetable that you would like
1 mango, peeled, seeded and cut in thin strips
A handful of fresh mint, coriander and basil leaves
A small handful of fresh chives

1. To make the assembly easy and fast, have all the filling ingredients ready in bowls or lined up on plates.
2. Off centre on a lettuce leaf, closer to you, place a small amount of each of the filling ingredients in a pile, finishing with the herb leaves. Roll up away from you, tucking in the sides as you go. To keep moist, envelop each roll in plastic wrap and place in a container. You may need to use toothpicks to secure the rolls. Repeat with the remaining lettuce leaves and filling ingredients. Refrigerate until serving time.
3. Fifteen to twenty minutes before serving time, bring the rolls and the spreadable sauce to room temperature. Serve 2 rolls per person. Enjoy!

What do 'chanterelles', 'morels' and 'oysters' have in common?
They are different varieties of mushrooms.

Salade de crevettes dans des coupes d'avocat
(Sweet Shrimp Salad in Avocado Cups)

Serves 4
Prep Time: 20-25 min.

The salad can be prepared ahead of time.
It is best to cut the avocados just before serving to prevent oxidation.

A- ½ lb small sweet shrimp, thawed and drained. (The variety I am referring to is found already shelled and cooked in the freezer at the grocery store. If you can't find it, use cooked prawns that you chop in small pieces.)
1 celery stalk, finely chopped
1 small red pepper, seeded, finely chopped
1 small green pepper, seeded, finely chopped
A handful of cherry tomatoes, finely chopped
Zest of half a lemon
2 tbsp each fresh parsley and basil, finely chopped

1 tbsp chives, finely cut with scissors
1 tsp fresh dill, finely chopped (or
a good pinch of dried dill)
A pinch of piment d'Espelette or hot red pepper
Celtic salt and pepper to taste
2 tbsp lemon juice
3-4 tbsp olive oil

B- 2 almost ripe avocados
1 tbsp lemon juice

1. In a mixing bowl, combine the **A** ingredients.
2. Cut the avocado in half, lengthwise. Remove and discard the stone. Brush some lemon juice on the flesh to prevent browning. Place each avocado on a small serving dish or bowl.
3. Spoon some of the salad mixture in the cavity of the avocado. Serve immediately.

47

Warming the Soul

Soups and Stews

I think a meal must start with a soup, steaming hot from the soup pot or refreshingly chilled from the refrigerator.
In my house, every day is a soup day, regardless of the weather and the temperature outside.
Sometimes, the soup is the meal!
It is a great way to showcase a variety of fresh produce, aromatic herbs from the garden and international spices.
A hot vegetable soup (with or without protein, clear or chunky)
makes a great light lunch that is comforting and enjoyable, yet satisfying.
Garnishes can offer great visual as well as taste buds appeal to each spoonful.
They can consist of chopped fruit (grapes, apple, pomegranate, etc.), chopped vegetables (cucumber,
tomatoes, pepper, etc.), roasted nuts, chopped herbs, roasted garlic or shallots, cooked shrimp, etc.
So, let your imagination soar and experiment with various combinations.

Did you know that Caterina de Medici was credited
with passing the art of fine cooking to the French?

Soupe aux poivrons rouges rôtis
(French Roasted Red Pepper Soup)

Serves 4-6
Prep Time: 15 min.
Roasting Time: 40 min.
Cooking Time: 15 min.

Colourful and sweet, this soup will satisfy you and your family on a cold winter day.

4 red peppers, halved and seeded	Celtic salt and pepper
8 large tomatoes, halved	1-2 tbsp maple syrup, if needed to balance the acidity
2 cups vegetable or organic chicken broth	2 tbsp fresh basil, shredded
Olive oil for brushing	Shaved parmesan to serve, if desired

1. Preheat oven to 400°F. Place the peppers skin side up on a baking sheet. In a baking dish, place the tomatoes flesh side up.
2. Brush the peppers and tomatoes with a little olive oil. Roast for 40 minutes, or until the pepper skins have charred spots and the tomatoes are soft.
3. To make peeling the pepper skins easy, allow the peppers to sweat for a few minutes by placing them in a paper bag, or in a bowl covered with plastic wrap. Let them cool; then, with a paper towel, rub off the charred skins.
4. Place the peppers and tomatoes in a food processor. Add a small amount of the chicken broth, and process until smooth.
5. Place the mixture in a saucepan with the remaining broth, and heat over medium heat until hot. Taste and adjust the season with salt and pepper. Stir in some maple syrup if you find it too acidic. Stir in basil. Serve with parmesan, if using.

Variation:

- For added natural sweetness, you can roast an onion, cut in half, along with the peppers, and process it with the peppers and tomatoes in the food processor.

Like a painter who uses a palette of colours,
you become a culinary artist by filling your plates with vibrantly coloured plant food.
Your dishes become unique works of art full of nourishing energy.

Soupe au fenouil et aux tomates
(French Fennel and Tomato Soup)

Serves 4-6
Prep Time: 15 min.
Cooking Time: 20-30 min.

I call this fat-free soup my *Spa Day Soup par excellence* because it is light, deliciously "clean" and nourishing. It is also great when you are not feeling well and you want something light, warm and nourishing to drink. It is excellent chilled on a hot summer day when you want something refreshing! If you like the licorice taste of fennel or anise bulb, you will love this simple soup!

6 cups of organic chicken broth
6 medium tomatoes or 8 small ones
1-2 celery, roughly chopped
1 fennel (or anise bulb), roughly chopped
10-12 fresh basil leaves

Celtic salt, black pepper and ground hot pepper to taste
Fresh parsley or basil, chopped, to garnish

1. In a large pot, heat the broth over medium-high heat.
2. With a sharp knife, cut an X on the bottom of each tomato and carve the stem area out.
3. When the broth is almost at the boiling point, gently drop the tomatoes in.
4. When the skin of the tomatoes around the X starts to separate from the flesh, remove the tomatoes from the broth and place in a large bowl to cool.
5. In the hot broth, add the celery, the fennel and the seasoning.
6. Peel the tomatoes and roughly chop them. Add to the broth, along with the basil leaves. Bring to a boil; then, simmer, covered, until fennel and celery are tender, and the soup is very fragrant.
7. The soup can be enjoyed as is, or puréed with a hand-held blender for a smooth version. You can also strain it through a sieve to create a light fragrant broth. Garnish with parsley or basil.

Greek Avgolemono Soup
(Egg and Lemon Soup)

Serves 6
Prep Time: 15 min.
Cooking Time: 30 min.

I bet you already have all these simple ingredients at home. You can make this easy recipe today!
This soup is so light and nourishing that it is almost medicinal!
It is ideal for when you are not feeling well, when you are feeling just great, and anywhere in between!

6 cups chicken broth
3 eggs
3 tbsp lemon juice

Celtic salt and pepper
1 tbsp each of fresh parsley and mint, chopped

1. In a saucepan, heat the chicken broth. In a medium size bowl, whisk the eggs and the lemon juice. As you continue turning the mixture with the whisk, gradually -- so not to cook the eggs -- add ½ cup of hot broth.
2. Pour this egg-y lemony broth in the saucepan. Simmer over low heat, taking care not to bring it to a boil. Season with salt and pepper. Garnish with chopped parsley and mint, and serve hot.

Serves 6
Prep Time: 15-20 min.
Cooking Time: 15-20 min.

This is my favourite Thai soup. It has everything to be a comforting and exciting meal in itself. Keep the seasoning interesting, vary the choices of vegetables and protein, and you have a new soup every time. Please note that the kaffir lime leaves and the lemongrass are only flavour enhancers, they are not to be eaten.

1 box of organic chicken broth
1 can regular coconut milk
1 tsp coconut sugar or sucanat
1 tsp hot chili sauce
3-4 kaffir lime leaves (or lime zest)
1 lemongrass stem, cut in 2-inch pieces
1 2-inch piece of ginger, peeled and cut in half
1 skinless, boneless, chicken breast, cut into thin strips

8-10 white mushrooms, sliced
1 large tomato, chopped
½ lb of shrimp, peeled, deveined
2 tbsp lime juice
2 tbsp fish sauce
¼ cup coriander, chopped
¼ cup fresh basil leaves, shredded

1. In a large pot, pour broth and coconut milk. Heat over medium heat. Whisk in sugar and chili sauce.
2. Add kaffir lime leaves, lemongrass and gingerroot. Bring to a boil; then, turn the heat down to simmer for a few minutes.
3. Add chicken, mushrooms, tomato and shrimp. Cook, stirring occasionally, until the chicken is cooked through and the shrimp are pink, about 4-6 minutes.
4. Stir in the lime juice and fish sauce. If you like, you can discard the kaffir lime leaves, the lemongrass and ginger pieces as they have fulfilled their purpose. Stir in the coriander and basil leaves. Spoon into bowls.

Variation:

- To increase the amount of vegetables, you can add chopped celery, sliced onion, a few chopped pieces of napa cabbage, some green beans, a few carrot rounds, etc.

According to Dr. Stone, equilibrium, as balanced energy flow, is the secret of well-being and healthy living:

"We are Physical Matter and have a physical body:
What we eat and drink, we become physically.
We are Emotion and have an emotional body:
What we feel and sense, we are emotionally.
We are Mind and have a mental body:
What we think and dwell upon, we are mentally."
(from his book, *Health Building, the Conscious Art of Living Well*)

Serves 6-8
Prep Time: 30 min.
Cooking Time: about 2 hours

This pasta-free soup is perfect for the end of summer or a cool autumn day when the hearty soup season is just beginning. You will enjoy this Italian soup the next day as well when the flavours have developed even more.

Flavouring Base:

¼ cup olive or coconut oil
1 large onion, finely chopped
1 large carrot, finely chopped

1 large celery stalk, finely chopped
Optional: 3-4 slices bacon or pancetta, finely chopped

Soup:

1 leek, white and light-green parts only,
rinsed well, cut into ¼-inch half moons
2 garlic cloves, minced
2 celery stalks, chopped in ¼-inch pieces
2 carrots, chopped in ¼-inch pieces
6-8 small red potatoes, cut in ¼-inch piece
1 zucchini, cut in ¼-inch pieces
1 cup green beans, trimmed, cut in ¾-inch pieces

1 14½-ounce can whole peeled tomatoes,
with their juice, cut with scissors
½ bunch of fresh spinach or kale leaves, chopped
2 cups of Savoy cabbage, thinly sliced
4 cups of vegetable or chicken broth
1 bay leaf
Celtic salt and pepper, and red pepper flakes to taste
To garnish: Fresh parsley and basil, chopped
Optional: Parmesan shavings

1. **The flavouring base:** Heat the oil in a large pot over medium-low heat. Add onion, carrot, celery, and bacon or pancetta, if using. Soften, stirring often, until they are deep golden brown, 20-25 minutes.
2. **The soup:** Add leek and garlic. Cook and stir often, until soft and fragrant, about 3-5 minutes.
3. Raise the heat to medium-high and add celery, carrots, potatoes, zucchini, and green beans. Cook, stirring often until brightly coloured, about 3-5 minutes. Stir in the tomatoes and juice, spinach, cabbage, broth, bay leaf and red pepper flakes. Season with salt and pepper. Bring to a boil. Reduce heat, cover and simmer for 1 hour or so. Serve with the herbs and the parmesan shavings.

The most beautiful and meaningful things in the world are felt by the heart.

Italian Fish and Seafood Soup

Serves 6-8
Prep Time: 30-40 min.
Cooking Time: 30 min. for the Stock, 45 min. for the Soup

This lovely dish, made with an assortment of fresh seafood and fish in a mildly spicy tomato broth, is similar to the French *bouillabaisse* and can be served as a hypo-caloric soup or a main course with a side salad. You can use any super-fresh fish and shellfish, and the results will be just as delectable and impressive. If you are using mussels, store them in a bowl in the refrigerator, covered with a damp towel until you are ready to make the soup. Before using them in the soup, pull off their scraggly "beard" with your fingers or a pair of pliers; then, scrub the shells with a brush. Wash and rinse several times in cold water. Discard the mussels that have a broken shell and any that don't open after cooking.

Shellfish Stock

1 lb fresh shrimp, shelled and deveined. Set the shrimp aside. Keep the shells to be used for this stock.

½ onion, peeled, quartered
1 carrot, peeled, cut into chunks
1 celery stalk, cut into chunks

In a saucepan, put the shrimp shells and cover with water. Bring to a boil; skim and discard the foam that comes to the surface. Add the vegetable chunks; bring to a boil; then, reduce the heat to a simmer. Cook for 30-45 minutes. Drain the liquid, and reserve. Discard the solids.

Soup Broth

2-3 tbsp olive or coconut oil or butter
2 medium onions, peeled, chopped
2 medium carrots, peeled, chopped
1 celery stalk, chopped
½ fennel or anise bulb, chopped
2 garlic cloves, peeled, minced
3 large bay leaves
Pinch of saffron
2 tsp fennel seeds
1 dried orange peel

2 cups each of rosé wine like Zinfandel
and **shellfish stock**
1 28-oz. can San Marzano diced
tomatoes, with their juice
1-2 tbsp tomato paste
3 tbsp each of fresh parsley and basil, chopped
2 tsp fresh oregano, chopped
Celtic salt and pepper
Crushed red pepper flakes

Heat the oil or butter in a large stockpot over medium heat. Add the onions, carrots, celery, and fennel. Stirring occasionally, cook until the vegetables are lightly golden, about 15-20 minutes. Add the garlic, bay leaves, saffron, fennel seeds and orange peel, and cook for 1 minute. Add the wine and bring to a boil, allowing the alcohol to evaporate. Add the **shellfish stock**, the tomatoes and their juice, tomato paste, herbs, salt, pepper, and red pepper flakes. Bring to a boil; reduce the heat and simmer for about 20 minutes.

Fish and Seafood

1 lb fresh mussels, well-scrubbed and de-bearded
1 lb fresh shrimp (reserved from above)
½ lb each of skinless salmon, halibut or other white
fish, bones removed, cut into 1½-inch cubes

½ lb crab meat, if desired
1 can baby clams, drained, liquid reserved

Stir the fish and seafood into the **soup broth**. Cover and simmer until the mussel shells open, the shrimp turn pink and the fish is opaque, about 4-6 minutes. Remove the pot from the heat. Taste and adjust the seasoning.

Garnishing

Combine and set aside: ½ cup **fresh parsley**, finely chopped, grated **zest of 1 orange**, 1-2 tbsp freshly squeezed **orange juice,** and 1 tbsp **olive oil.**

Serve the soup in deep bowls with a spoonful of the garnishing on top. Provide empty bowls to collect the discarded mussel shells.

Lily Ma's Poached Chicken Soup

Serves 4-6
Prep Time: 10 min.
Cooking Time: 45 min. to 1 hour

Philip's mother, Lily ("Ma" is for "Mother"; I like to call her Lily Ma because it has a nice ring to it, and she likes it), used to make wonderfully comforting Chinese soups. She used various Chinese ingredients and produce; some I knew, many I didn't. When Philip and I went to Chinatown to visit his family, Lily Ma often gave me interesting soup ingredients, fresh and dried, to take home. With Philip and his sisters Shirley and Rita translating, I was able to understand what to do with the ingredients and write Lily Ma's recipes. As you can expect, there are no exact measurements! Sadly, Philip's parents had to move to a retirement home, and Lily Ma doesn't cook anymore. There are only a few of her soups that I can replicate. I am grateful to have received some of her recipes and techniques so I can make them for her and her husband when we go visit them.
(Below is a picture of Philip and Lily Ma in her kitchen where many wonderful meals were made and enjoyed.)

For this recipe, I use her poaching technique that provides plenty of juicy meat and a very flavourful broth, without any fuss. The soup is served in small bowls with a little bit of each solid ingredient and the fragrant broth.

1. In a large stock pot that can hold **a whole chicken** comfortably, pour enough cold water to come about halfway up the sides. Add some Celtic salt, cover and bring to a boil.
2. In the meantime, wash the chicken. Place in its cavity, **2-3 star anise** and **2-3 slices of ginger**.
3. When the water is boiling, carefully ease the chicken into the hot water. Bring back to a boil, skimming the foam that comes up to the surface of the water. Reduce the heat to medium and cook for 5-10 minutes.
4. Turn off the heat, cover the stock pot and let the chicken cook in the hot liquid for about 45 minutes.
5. Once cooked, carefully lift the chicken out and transfer to a large bowl or serving platter. The meat can then be carved out, and the broth used for soups.

Tune into yourself to 'know' your daily nourishment needs
so you don't rely on anyone's rules and opinions regarding the food you should (or shouldn't) eat.

Marie-Claire's Floral Chicken Soup

Serves 6
Prep Time: 10 min.
Cooking Time: 45 min. to 1 hour

Inspired by Lily Ma's technique, I have created this version of an equally juicy chicken with a floral and fruity broth. You can serve the meat and the carrots with the **dipping sauce**.

1. In a large stockpot that can hold **a whole chicken** comfortably, pour enough cold water to come about halfway up the sides. Add some Celtic salt, cover and bring to a boil.
2. In the meantime, wash the chicken. Place in its cavity ½ **bunch of fresh coriander**.
3. When the water is boiling, carefully ease the chicken into the hot water. Bring back to a boil, skimming the foam that comes up to the surface of the water. Add **1 dried orange peel, 2 star anise, 1 slice of ginger, 2-3 kaffir lime leaves** and/or ½ **lemongrass stick, a large handful of goji berries**, and 2-3 peeled carrots cut in small rounds. Reduce the heat to medium and cook for 5-10 minutes.
4. Turn off the heat, cover the stock pot and let the chicken cook in the hot liquid for about 45 minutes.

5. Once cooked, carefully lift the chicken out and transfer to a large bowl or serving platter. The meat can then be carved out, and the broth divided among soup bowls.

Dipping Sauce:

Combine all ingredients in a screw-top glass jar, and shake vigorously. Refrigerate the unused potion for up to 2 days. This sauce is great with grilled shrimp

1 tbsp fresh coriander, chopped
¼ cup rice wine vinegar
1 tbsp maple syrup
1 tsp lime zest

2-3 tsp lime juice
2 tsp sesame oil
1 tsp each of hot red pepper flakes
and toasted sesame seeds

Lily Ma's Carrot Soup

Serves 4-6
Prep Time: 15 min.
Cooking Time: 2-2½ hours

When my parents used to visit us in Toronto, we often met with Philip's family for dinner in Chinatown. The two mothers, walking arm in arm, were almost inseparable as they attempted to communicate with one another. Frequently, they were calling on Philip and me for translation assistance. Lily Ma would tell Philip in Chinese what she wanted to say to my mother, he would translate it to me in English, and I would interpret it in French to my mother. Then, we would repeat the process in reverse with my mother's reply in French.

Here is another one of Lily Ma's delicious and easy-to-make soup.

Several pork, chicken or beef bones (or a combination).
I like to use bone-in chicken thighs.
6 dried shiitake mushrooms, reconstituted in hot water
1 dried mandarin peel, reconstituted in hot water
Several carrots, peeled, cut in rounds

A couple slices of fresh gingerroot
A few pieces of water chestnuts,
fresh and peeled, or canned
Celtic salt

Fill a large stockpot to three-quarters of its capacity with water. Add the bones and bring to a boil. Skim the impurities that rise to the surface. Add the rest of the ingredients. Cover and simmer for about 2 hours. Discard the bones and serve.

Chinese Short Rib Stew
(*Ngaou Nam*)

Serves 6-8
Prep Time: 15-20 min.
Cooking Time: 2 hours

This is another inexpensive and nutritious dish from Lily Ma's recipe collection.
Philip and I love to make it in the winter. The sweetness of the broth imparted from the vegetables
and the orange peel makes this stew very tasty and comforting on a cold day. It is Philip's favourite stew!

3 lbs short ribs cut in between the bones
2 tbsp Celtic salt

10-12 carrots, peeled and cut in large chunks
4-5 large potatoes, scrubbed and cut in large chunks

1 2-inch piece of fresh ginger, peeled and cut in chunks   ½ regular cabbage, cut in quarters
2 dried orange peels

1. Fill a large stockpot to two-thirds of its capacity with cold water. Add the salt and bring to a boil.
2. Add the short ribs and bring back to a boil. Skim the impurities that rise to the surface. Cover and simmer for 1 hour.
3. Add the rest of the ingredients except the cabbage. Bring back to a boil; then, simmer, uncovered, for 45 minutes or so, until the carrots are tender and the meat is fork-tender. Add the cabbage and cook for 15 minutes or so, until the cabbage has softened.
4. Serve in bowls with plenty of broth and enjoy!

We all need something to do,
someone to love,
and something to look forward to.

Old-fashioned Beef Bone Broth

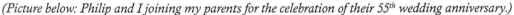

This tasty universal concoction is a great base for soups. My parents told me that they often took part in the cooking and bone broth making with their parents. Most of the broths were made in the fall from any bone, especially those that contain marrow (beef, lamb, pork). My father told me that his family and community even used bones from deer and moose, as they believed that the wild animals had more flavour and therapeutic properties than the farm animals.

(Picture below: Philip and I joining my parents for the celebration of their 55th wedding anniversary.)

The marrow was crushed, and melted in the broth, to be strained later. The broths, made in late fall, were boiled, and then simmered for hours, filling the house with their aromatic steam. Sometimes a few herbs and celery leaves were added for extra flavour. Since there were no refrigerators or freezers at the time, the broths, once transferred to sterilized jars or jugs, were stored in outdoor sheds to be available for the Christmas and New Year's meal preparations, where they became part of soups, sauces, meat pies, stews, and *cipaille* -- a French-Canadian festive dish made with various meats, wild and farm-raised, or mixed seafood.

These simple broths were often given to whoever was not feeling well and needed to be "fortified". Everyone knew that a potent, hot broth held some "magical" healing properties and could relieve the discomfort of a head cold, among many other things, while providing much needed fortifying nutrients.

As I mentioned earlier, Philip's mother, Lily Ma, used to make amazingly delicious soups in which she, too, used any bones she could find to create flavourful bases. The Chinese people believe that one can make a tasty soup out of anything, and that it has some healing properties.

Every time Philip and I used to go for a visit, which was a weekly occurrence sometimes, there was always a freshly-made, yummy soup waiting for us! I have tried to replicate some of them following her instructions. I must admit that mine don't taste as good as hers! I know that it was her old pots, the special Chinese ingredients, and her personal touch that made her soups so great.

Beef Bone Soup

You will need 3-5 lbs beef soup bones with marrow (the edible, soft, fatty substance found in the cavity of long bones) and some meat still attached, washed. Plenty of water.

1. In a large stockpot or slow cooker, add the bones; pour enough water to cover them.
2. Bring to a boil; skim and discard the foam that comes to the surface.
3. Turn the heat down and simmer for at least 6 hours or more (the longer the better). Cover if using a slow cooker.

If you make a large batch and can't use all of it at once, you can freeze the surplus in 2-cup plastic containers, label and date. You can also freeze the broth in ice cube trays. Once the cubes are frozen, transfer them to a freezer bag, label and date. The frozen broth can be thawed in a pot on the stove when you need a flavourful liquid for a soup, a sauce or a dish.

Loading Up on the Greens

Salads and Vegetable Dishes

My favorite section of any cookbook! (Other than the desserts section, of course!) Raw from the garden, steamed, sautéed, braised, boiled, grilled, roasted; they are all so *good*! These brightly coloured wonders from the earth are the foundation of the spa cuisine.

I see good-quality nourishment as daily investments toward my long-term immunity, comfort, and longevity filled with steady health. Nothing can imitate products from Mother Nature and claim to be as good, tasty, effective and healing. Since we are creatures of Nature, it makes sense that what keeps us alive and well comes from Nature.

As with the soups, I feel that every day is vegetable day! Produce provide plenty of colours, textures and flavours to make a dish quite interesting for any meal. I often have steamed vegetables or a salad for breakfast. It prevents me from going after the carbs. Here is what I keep in mind when I plan a meal: more fresh leafy greens, less animal protein; more fresh produce, less dairy; more nuts and seeds, less salt and sweetener.

Feel comfortable to eat large quantities of raw and cooked vegetables for lunch and dinner, and even breakfast! They are Nature's remedy for many health issues as they are filled with phytonutrients, antioxidants, fiber, vitamins, minerals, proteins, and water -- all essential elements to reach and maintain vibrant health and longevity. Their bright colours and unique shapes allow us to create dishes that are full of irresistible visual appeal. And remember, when you fill up on plant food, there isn't much room for unhealthy foods that create cravings, addictions and overeating.

A bonus: vegetables are naturally **hypo-caloric**!

Indian Roasted Brussels Sprouts

Serves 4-6
Prep Time: 5 min.
Cooking Time: 30 min.

While roasting, the outer leaves become crispy and caramelized,
deliciously enhancing this very often ignored vegetable.

1 tbsp oil	Pinch of Celtic salt
½ tsp cumin	4 cups (1 lb) Brussels sprouts, trimmed and cut in half
1 tsp garam masala	

1. Preheat the oven to 425°F. In a large bowl, combine all ingredients. Toss to coat the sprouts with the oil and spices evenly. In a single layer, place the sprouts cut side down on a baking sheet.
2. Place in oven and roast about 15 minutes. If they are not browning at the end of the roasting time, return to oven for another 15 minutes. Roast until they are cooked to your liking: softer texture, tender or firmer.

Confetti Melon Salsa

Makes 2½ cups
Prep Time: 30 min.

This festive confetti-like salsa is beautiful and delectable.
It can be served as a side dish to accompany grilled fish or chicken, or as an appetizer, a snack,
and even as part of breakfast. I served it once as an appetizer for an afternoon tea party.
My guests were so pleased with the vibrant colours and the refreshing flavours that they asked for seconds
even before reaching for the other dishes!
It is quite delicious with only one melon variety. Cut all the ingredients in very small cubes (¼ inch) like confetti.
Choose any herb you like or have on hand, adding them to the salsa just before serving time.

1½ cups ripe melons of different varieties
and colours, cut in ¼-inch cubes
½ red pepper, cut in very small pieces
½ yellow pepper, cut in very small pieces
½ orange pepper, cut in very small pieces
½ English cucumber, cut in very small pieces

½ small jalapeño pepper, seeded and finely diced
2 tbsp lime juice and some zest
1 tbsp olive oil
Pinch of Celtic salt
1 tbsp each chopped mint, coriander, basil and chives

Place the melon cubes in a large bowl. Add the peppers, cucumber, jalapeño, lime juice and zest, olive oil, salt and herbs. Gently toss and serve.

Black and Green Salad

Serves 4
Prep Time: 25-30 min.

The bright blue-black colour from the blackberries against the light green of the cucumber and the apple makes this salad quite attractive and unusual. You will find this salad refreshing for its juicy flavours and crisp textures.

Dressing:

In a screw-top glass jar, combine the following ingredients. Screw the lid on and shake vigorously.
Taste and adjust the seasoning if needed.

4 tsp lime juice and some zest
4 tsp olive oil
2 tsp each of raspberry vinegar and honey or maple syrup
½ tsp Dijon mustard

Chopped chives
Pinch of Celtic salt
Optional: ½ tsp poppy seeds

Salad:

2 cups of arugula
1 cup blackberries
½ English cucumber, julienned

½ Granny Smith, julienned
Chopped mint and coriander

In a salad bowl, combine the salad ingredients. Toss with some of the dressing and serve immediately.

I'm not overweight, I'm just not tall enough.

Caprese Salad

Serves 4
Prep Time: 15 min.

My favourite Italian classic salad! I have had several versions, from the outstandingly delicious and appealing to… well, quite disappointing. The following is my version of a salad I enjoyed in Rome where I find that the tomatoes are the best on the planet! I hope you will like it, too. The key to this salad is the very fresh red, white and green ingredients. It is an ideal dish to make when there is an abundance of tomatoes and basil at the end of the summer. If you don't care for the anchovies, you know what to do. If you don't want the cheese, you know what to do, too!

4 cups of fresh arugula or other lettuce leaves
6-8 medium-size tomatoes, sliced
2-3 cups of bocconcini, sliced
¼ red onion, thinly sliced
Anchovy fillets, as many as you like, drained

1 cup fresh basil leaves
Balsamic vinegar
Extra-virgin olive oil
A pinch of Celtic salt and pepper

On individual serving plates, arrange arugula, tomatoes, bocconcini, red onion, anchovies, and basil leaves. Drizzle some balsamic vinegar and olive oil. Season with salt and pepper to taste.

Fennel and Orange Salad

Serves 4
Prep Time: 15 min.

This is a great salad when the fennel is in season. It is easy and quick to prepare. The anise and orange flavours, as well as the green and bright orange colours, will be a hit at your dinner table. I often use blood oranges or Cara Cara oranges when they become available. Their brighter red-orange colour and sweet juice make this salad even tastier and appealing. Visit my website www.olivestolychees.com for a demonstration on how to cut *suprêmes*.

1 large fennel bulb or anise
2-3 oranges, zested and cut into *suprêmes*
Fresh green olives, pitted and sliced
Olive oil

Chopped parsley
Celtic salt and pepper
Optional: toasted pine nuts

Cut the "fingers" from the fennel and discard, keeping only the best fronds or fern for garnishing. Peel the outer layer of the fennel if it is not intact or fresh looking. Cut the bulb in half, core and slice in thin 1-inch pieces. Chop the fronds. Place fennel pieces and fronds in a salad bowl. Add the orange zest and the *suprêmes*, olive slices, parsley, salt and pepper. Drizzle some olive oil and toss. Taste the olive oil-orange juice mix and add more orange juice if needed. Sprinkle some pine nuts, if using, and serve immediately. If you don't plan on serving the salad right away, keep it refrigerated without the pine nuts until serving time. Sprinkle the pine nuts just before serving.

Steamed Broccoli and Carrots

Serves 4
Prep Time: 10 min.
Cooking Time: 15 min.

This is my Mother's recipe that I make when I don't have much time or inspiration to cook, and I need one more vegetable dish for dinner. You can use cauliflower as well. No fuss!

2 heads of broccoli, cut in florets
3-4 medium carrots, peeled, cut
diagonally in ¼-inch slices
1 small garlic clove, minced or rubbed on a microplane
2 tbsp olive oil
1 tbsp apple cider vinegar
Celtic salt and pepper

To garnish: chopped fresh parsley

Steam the broccoli florets for a few minutes until they are bright green and fork tender. Transfer to a serving bowl. Steam the carrots slices until they are fork tender. Add to the broccoli bowl. Add garlic, oil and vinegar. Season and toss to combine. Sprinkle with parsley.

Moroccan Blood Oranges and Beets Salad

Serves 4
Prep Time: 15 min.

This beautiful orange-red salad is so delicious when the blood oranges and the pomegranates are in season.
For a demonstration on how to extract the "juicy rubies" out of a pomegranate,
visit my website www.olivestolychees.com.

Salad:

1 head of lettuce of your choice (romaine,
red leaf), cut in bite size
3 blood oranges or regular oranges,
zested, peeled and cut in rounds
2-3 beets, cooked, peeled and cut in thin slices

1 cup of pomegranate seeds or dried cranberries
1 cup cherry tomatoes, cut in half
A handful of fresh mint and parsley leaves
⅓ cup almond slivers or pistachios, lightly toasted

Minty-cumin Vinaigrette:

In a screw-top glass jar, combine the following ingredients. Screw the lid on and shake vigorously.
Taste and adjust the flavours to suit your palate.

1 small garlic clove, minced
¾ cup of extra-virgin olive oil
2½ tbsp each of red wine vinegar,
cider vinegar and lemon juice
1½ tsp Dijon mustard

¼ to ½ cup chopped fresh mint
1 tbsp chives, finely cut with scissors
1½ tsp ground cumin
A pinch of Celtic salt

Cover the bottom of a large platter with the lettuce. Arrange the blood orange slices and the beet slices on top of the lettuce. Scatter the tomato halves, the pomegranate seeds, and the mint and parsley leaves over the orange and beet slices. When ready to serve, sprinkle the nuts and drizzle some of the vinaigrette.

Serves 4
Grilling Time: 10-15 min.
Prep Time: 15 min.

I find this salad interesting for its textures and colourful appeal. If it doesn't get eaten the day I make it, the next day, I stir-fry the squid in a hot pan with some oil for a few minutes. Then, I add the rest of the leftover ingredients to the pan and toss for a minute or two until hot and the lettuce and the spinach leaves have wilted.

4 fresh whole squids, washed
½ lemon
4 cups fresh lettuce leaves, washed and cut
2 cups fresh baby spinach leaves
4 medium-sized juicy tomatoes, quartered
2 large handfuls of green beans, steamed
½ can white beans (optional)
1 cup pitted olives of your choice

4-6 anchovy fillets, drained and coarsely chopped
A handful of fresh basil leaves, torn
3-4 tbsp olive oil
Salt and pepper
1 tsp hot pepper flakes

1. Season the squids with salt and pepper. On the barbecue or under the broiler, cook the squids until tender. Set aside on a plate and squirt some lemon juice over them.
2. In a large bowl or on 4 individual serving plates, distribute the lettuce and spinach leaves. Scatter the tomatoes, green beans, white beans if using, olives, anchovies and basil leaves.
3. Cut the squid legs from their bodies. (You can decide what to do with the bodies.) Scatter the legs over the salad ingredients. Drizzle the oil, some lemon juice and lightly season with salt, pepper and hot pepper flakes. Gently toss to coat.

Variations:

- Instead of white beans, you can use fresh fava beans that you steam and shell.
- For added flavour and a creamy texture, you can add 8-12 roasted garlic cloves that you squash in the oil and tomato juices.

It's funny how a great meal can bring people together and make everyone happy.

Fuyu Persimmons and Hazelnut Salad

Serves 4
Prep Time: 20-25 min.

A **fuyu persimmon** (or Sharon fruit) is a sweet orange fruit that can be purchased, when in season, in most Asian grocery stores. Cut off the stem, and slice in wedges. The skin is a little firm and gives an appealing texture to this delicious fruit.

Salad:

4 cups each of fresh arugula and frisée
4 fuyu persimmons, stemmed, cut into thin wedges
1 cup of thin cucumber slices
½ cup pomegranate seeds

½ cup hazelnuts or pistachios, toasted
1 tbsp each of fresh chives and parsley, chopped
Optional: feta or Boursin or other
soft cheese of your choice

Vinaigrette:

In a screw-top glass jar, combine the following ingredients. Screw the lid on and shake vigorously.

1 tsp each of shallot and gingerroot,
finely grated with a microplane
1 tbsp each of orange zest, orange juice
and honey or maple syrup

1 tsp Dijon mustard
2 tbsp each of apple cider vinegar and olive oil
Celtic salt and pepper to taste

On individual serving plates, mound about 1 cup each of arugula and frisée leaves. Scatter fuyu persimmon wedges, cucumber slices, pomegranate seeds, nuts, and herbs. Scatter the Boursin in clumps, if using. Drizzle the vinaigrette.

Rustic Salad with Watermelon, Cucumber and Mint

Serves 4-6
Prep Time: 10-15 min.

I like this refreshing salad all year long as the ingredients are available throughout the year. You can make it up to 2 hours before serving time, and keep it covered in the refrigerator.

1 English cucumber
¼ of a large seedless watermelon
Zest of 1 lime
Juice of 1 lime
⅔ cup fresh mint, torn or roughly chopped
2-3 tbsp extra-virgin olive oil
Celtic salt and pepper

⅓ cup feta, crumbled (optional)
Extra fresh mint leaves to garnish

1. Slice the cucumber in half lengthwise. Scrape out and discard the seeds if you like. Cut the cucumber in small chunks and place in a large bowl or a platter.
2. Cut the watermelon in small chunks and add to the cucumber.
3. Stir in the lime zest and juice, mint, olive, salt and pepper. Top with the feta if using. Garnish with the mint leaves.
4. For extra flavour, you can add a few chopped tomatoes and fresh basil leaves to the mix. Instead of lime zest and juice, drizzle a few teaspoons of balsamic vinegar over the salad.

Focusing on eating well instead of dieting is more of a lifestyle than a short-term project.
Put your attention and energy on building your health instead of worrying about your weight.

Chinese Stir-fried Vegetables

Serves 4
Prep Time: 15-20 min.
Cooking Time: 10 min.

This crunchy and colourful dish is great with grilled chicken, beef or salmon.

1½ cups fresh snow peas, trimmed
½ cup each of broccoli and cauliflower florets
2 tbsp olive oil or coconut oil
1 cup each carrots and celery, cut into short, thin sticks

1 cup zucchini, cut into short, thin sticks
6-8 white mushrooms, sliced
1 cup bean sprouts

1-2 tbsp organic tamari
Ground black pepper
To garnish: sesame seeds, white and/or black

1. In a pot of hot salted water, cook the snow peas, broccoli and cauliflower for about 3 minutes to soften. Drain and reserve.
2. In a hot wok or a frying pan, over medium heat, warm the oil and stir-fry the snow peas, broccoli, cauliflower, carrots and celery sticks for about 2-3 minutes. Add the zucchini and mushrooms and cook for another 2-3 minutes.
3. Add the bean sprouts, the tamari and the pepper. Serve with sesame seeds sprinkled over the vegetables.

Variations:

- Other vegetable options for colour, texture and taste: red pepper strips, green or yellow beans, or tomato.
- Different flavourings: chopped onion, minced garlic, chopped ginger, chopped shallot, etc.
- More garnishes: fresh coriander leaves, caramelized onion slices, hot pepper flakes, roasted cashews, etc.

Oven-dried Tomatoes

Makes 2 cups
Prep Time: 10 min.
Cooking Time: 2-2½ hours

These delicious, thick slices of savory-sweet tomato candy can be used as appetizers on *hors d'œuvre* or as a sandwich filler. They can also be diced and tossed in a fresh salad or in a tomato sauce with fresh herbs.
It is a great way to use tomatoes when there is an abundance of them at the end of the summer.

6-8 tomatoes, any kind, any size
1½ tsp Celtic salt
2 tsp black pepper
2 tsp cane sugar or sucanat

½ tsp each of fresh thyme leaves, parsley
leaves, mint leaves, finely chopped
Olive oil

1. Preheat the oven to 250°F. Line a baking sheet with a piece of parchment paper.
2. Cut the tomatoes crosswise in thick slices of about ¼ inch, and place them on the parchment paper.
3. In a small bowl, mix the salt, pepper, sugar and herbs together.
4. Drizzle the tomato slices with some oil, and sprinkle with the salt-herb mixture.
5. Slow roast for 2-2½ hours, until they are a bit dehydrated, crispier, almost leather-like.

Day-After-a-Feast Salad

Serves 4
Prep Time: 20 min.

This is a salad I often make the day after a big dinner for family and friends
when there is plenty of leftover roasted or grilled meats and vegetables.
The abundant and delicious leftovers give us ample supplies for many tasty dishes like this salad,
sauces, omelets, and Paleo sandwiches with lettuce leaves instead of bread slices.
There are no exact measurements, use what you have on hand. It will be scrumptious!

Vinaigrette:

In a screw-top glass jar, combine the following ingredients.
Screw the lid on and shake vigorously. Taste and adjust the flavours to your liking.

1 garlic clove, grated with a microplane
3 tbsp red wine vinegar or apple cider vinegar
3 tbsp extra-virgin olive oil
1 tbsp maple syrup

Salad:

Any leftover meat (chicken, veal, beef, lamb),
grilled or roasted, cut into small cubes
¼ small red onion, thinly sliced or chopped
3 tomatoes, chopped
1 celery stalk, chopped
1-2 red pepper, grilled or roasted,
peeled and chopped
1 orange or yellow pepper, grilled or
roasted, peeled and chopped
1 zucchini, grilled or roasted, chopped
6-7 cornichons, chopped
3 tbsp capers, rinsed and drained
1 garlic clove, minced

½ tsp Dijon mustard
Fresh chives, cut with scissors
Celtic salt and pepper

¼ cup each of fresh parsley and basil, chopped
Celtic salt and pepper

Put all the salad ingredients in a large salad bowl and mix well. Add the vinaigrette and toss. Cover and refrigerate for 20-30 minutes before serving. Enjoy with a soup or as a side dish. It tastes just as great the day after!

Caraway Cabbage

Serves 4-6
Prep Time: 5 min.
Cooking Time: 15-20 min.

2 tbsp butter or coconut oil
1 onion, sliced
1 tsp caraway seeds
Pinch of red pepper flakes

1 small Savoy cabbage, cored, finely sliced
Celtic salt and pepper
Optional: add 1 tsp curry powder in step 2.

1. Melt the butter or oil in a large saucepan over medium heat. Add the onion slices and cook for 3-4 minutes.
2. Add the caraway seeds and pepper flakes. Stir and add the cabbage.
3. Season with salt and pepper and cook for a couple of minutes, until wilted and shiny.
4. Add 3-4 tbsp of water, cover and cook over low heat for 12-15 minutes or until tender, stirring occasionally.

Pineapple and Macadamia Salsa

Makes 1½ cups
Prep Time: 15 min.
Optional Grilling Time: 10 minutes

This Polynesian salsa is great as a topping or a side dish for grilled meats and burgers. If you can't find macadamia nuts or would prefer to use other nuts, toasted pine nuts or pumpkin seeds would work quite well, too.

½ pineapple, quartered
½ cup unsalted macadamia, lightly toasted and chopped
½ cup red bell pepper, diced

<table>
<tr><td>½ cup green pepper, diced</td><td>2 tbsp coriander, finely chopped</td></tr>
<tr><td>2-3 tbsp red onion, finely chopped</td><td>1-2 tsp jalapeño pepper, finely chopped</td></tr>
<tr><td>1 tbsp lime zest</td><td>1 garlic clove, finely chopped</td></tr>
<tr><td>2 tbsp lime juice</td><td>Celtic salt and pepper</td></tr>
</table>

Chop the pineapple into ¼-inch cubes. Toss with all the ingredients in a mixing bowl. Season to taste.

Variation:

If you are already grilling some meat on the barbecue or in a grill pan and you want to add a different dimension to this salsa, grill the pineapple quarters 4 minutes on each side until dark grilled marks appear; then, chop them in small cubes to be tossed with the salsa.

Did you know that the macadamia nut is native to Hawaii?

Carrot and Parsnip Mash

Serves 4
Prep Time: 10-15 min.
Cooking Time: 25-30 min.

Who doesn't like mash or vegetable purée?
I love their creamy-smooth texture, their chunky texture, their rustic texture; I love them all!
With the leftovers, I often add crumbled cooked fish or crab meat, a beaten egg, ground flaxseeds, fried onions, herbs and spices, and turn the whole mixture into cakes to be quickly pan-fried, and then baked.
Served with a salsa as a topping and a fresh side salad, it is a great colourful meal. Yum!

<table>
<tr><td>4 medium parsnips, peeled, hard centre core removed, cut into ½-inch dice</td><td>½ cup chicken broth</td></tr>
<tr><td>5-6 carrots, peeled, cut into ¼-inch dice</td><td>½ cup water</td></tr>
<tr><td>1 small garlic clove, finely grated on a microplane</td><td>Celtic salt and pepper to taste</td></tr>
<tr><td>2 tbsp butter or olive oil</td><td>**To garnish:** 1 tbsp chives, finely cut with scissors</td></tr>
</table>

1. In a saucepan, combine parsnips, carrots, garlic, butter or oil, broth, water and salt and pepper. Cover and cook until vegetables are tender, about 25-30 minutes. Let cool for a while.
2. Transfer to a food processor and purée. Spoon into a serving bowl and garnish with chives.

Variation:

You can add a cooked and mashed Yukon Gold potato or a sweet potato to the puréed mixture above.

Mango-cado Salad

Serves 4
Prep Time: 15-20 min.
Toasting Time: 5 min.

This salad, with its bitter leaves, is perfect when served as an accompaniment to a rich dish.

Salad:

<table>
<tr><td>1 large ripe mango, peeled and sliced thinly</td><td>A handful of chives, chopped</td></tr>
<tr><td>2 cups of an assortment of bitter salad leaves like endive, radicchio, arugula, frisée, baby spinach</td><td>¼ English cucumber, cut in thin half moons</td></tr>
<tr><td>1 cup cherry tomatoes, halved</td><td>¼ cup toasted pine nuts</td></tr>
<tr><td></td><td>1 large ripe avocado</td></tr>
</table>

Dressing:

In a screw-top glass jar, combine the following ingredients.
Screw the lid on and shake vigorously to emulsify.

4 tbsp olive oil
2 tbsp orange juice
1 tsp Dijon mustard

1-2 tsp maple syrup or honey
Celtic salt and pepper

Rinse the salad leaves, pat them dry and place in a serving bowl. Arrange the mango slices, tomatoes, chives and cucumber. Cut the avocado crosswise, and remove the stone. With a spoon, lift the green flesh out of the shell. Cut the flesh in thin slices. Arrange them on the salad. Sprinkle over the nuts. Drizzle some dressing, toss the salad gently and serve.

Flying Protein

Chicken and Turkey

Who doesn't like chicken?
It is such a popular protein choice everywhere in the world, and on all restaurant menus.
It is easy to raise, to cook, and it provides tasty lean meat.

Mediterranean Braised Chicken

Serves 4-6
Prep Time: 5-10 min.
Cooking Time: 40 min.

This chicken dish is quite simple and flavourful. You can serve it with a side dish of roasted vegetables and a green salad. You may even have enough for some leftovers!

8 organic chicken legs, separated
into thighs and drumsticks
2 tbsp olive oil
1 large onion, finely chopped
4-5 garlic cloves, thinly sliced
1¼ cups chicken broth
3 tbsp tomato paste
⅓ cup black olives or Kalamata, pitted and halved
4-6 wide strips of orange zest of about ½" x 2"

Celtic salt and pepper
Freshly chopped parsley for garnish

1. Wash and pat dry the chicken pieces. Season with salt and pepper.
2. In a Dutch oven, heat 1 tbsp oil over medium-high heat. Working in batches, brown the chicken pieces. Using tongs, turn the chicken pieces as each side becomes golden brown, about 5-8 minutes. Transfer to a platter.

3. Add remaining tablespoon of oil to the Dutch oven. Cook onion, stirring frequently, until the onion is softened, about 5-7 minutes. Add the garlic slices and cook for a few minutes.
4. Add the broth, tomato paste, olives and orange zest strips. Season with salt and pepper. Bring to a boil.
5. Return chicken to the Dutch oven. Cover and simmer, turning the chicken once or twice, until tender, about 20 minutes or so. Serve hot, sprinkled with parsley.

Variation:

Omit the olives; instead, add 1 stick of cinnamon, the juice of an orange, 1 tbsp maple syrup and 1 tsp harissa or hot pepper sauce.

Pot-au-feu Platter
("Pot on the Fire")

Serves 6
Prep Time: 20-30 min.
Cooking Time: 30 min.

A *pot-au-feu* is a very basic, spa dish that provides soup (the broth), boiled meat (beef or chicken), and vegetables. It is prepared in a big pot in which all the ingredients are cooked together in water with added flavourings. It is, then, gently simmered over steady low heat to preserve the subtle flavour of each ingredient. In this low and moist heat of the pot, the simmering ingredients become extra tender and fragrant. Because it is such a hypo-caloric, healthy and tasty meal in itself, you and your guests will feel comforted and satisfied - even virtuous! Your guests will give you smiles of appreciation. This dish can be served hot or chilled over romaine lettuce leaves with the vinaigrette below. I like to start with a bowl of the hot broth.

Bouquet Garni:

Wrap in a cheese cloth the following ingredients:
2-3 bay leaves, 8 black peppercorns, 2 sprigs of thyme, a handful of parsley
Tie with a kitchen twine and set aside.

Pot-au-feu:

1 tbsp butter
24 pearl onions, peeled☺
12 whole cloves
2 leeks, only the pale green part, cleaned and cut in half
4 celery stalks, cut in chunks
2 parsnips, peeled and cut into chunks
24 white mushrooms, cut in half
24 baby carrots, scrubbed, or 4 large carrots, peeled, and cut in chunks
12 florets each of cauliflower and broccoli
3 boneless, skinless chicken breasts (about 1 lb)

2½ cups chicken broth
2 large handfuls each of green beans and yellow wax beans, trimmed
A handful of parsley
2-3 sprigs of thyme
Celtic salt and pepper
18 very small potatoes, scrubbed, and cut into chunks.
In order to prevent the broth from becoming "cloudy", it is best to boil the potatoes separately in salted water until tender for 15-20 minutes, and drain.

Accompaniments For the Hot Version:

gherkins
various mustards
pickles

pickled beets
horseradish, if using beef
red current jam as used in Eastern France

Vinaigrette For the Chilled Version:

In a screw-top glass jar, combine the following ingredients.
Screw the lid on and shake vigorously:

3 tbsp wine vinegar	3 tbsp olive oil
2 tbsp Dijon mustard	Celtic salt and pepper
2 tbsp honey	

Pot-au-feu:

1. Heat butter in a large pot over medium heat. Stud half the pearl onions with 1 clove. Add to the pot with the rest of the onions, leeks, celery, parsnips, mushrooms, and carrots; toss to coat.
2. Add cauliflower; stir to combine. Add chicken breasts, broth, the bouquet garni and enough water to cover the contents of the pot.
3. Bring to a boil; reduce to a gentle simmer. Cover the pot. Cook until vegetables are almost tender, about 15-20 minutes. Add the broccoli, the green and yellow beans, and the fresh herbs; cook until the broccoli and the beans are cooked, the vegetables are just tender and still brightly coloured, and the chicken is cooked through, about 10-15 minutes. Remove the herbs.
4. **If serving hot**, transfer vegetables and the potatoes onto a platter, and arrange by category. Discard the bouquet garni. Cut the chicken breasts in thick slices and arrange in the centre of the platter amongst the vegetables. Serve in bowls with the flavourful hot broth on the side. Season with Celtic sea salt and pepper. Serve with the accompaniments. Garnish with fresh parsley. (It is great when a little bit of mustard meets some of the broth in your bowl: a lovely sauce with a bit of a kick!)
5. **If serving chilled**, line the platter with fresh lettuce leaves of your choice (romaine, red leaf, spinach). Transfer the vegetables to the platter, arrange by category, and let cool to room temperature. Slice the chicken breasts in thin pieces or shreds, and toss in a bowl with ⅓ of the vinaigrette. Add the chicken mixture in the centre of the platter. Drizzle the rest of the vinaigrette over the cooled vegetables. Season with salt and pepper. Serve with the accompaniments. Garnish with fresh parsley.

☺To peel the pearl onions more easily (and without any tears!), soak them in a bowl of very hot water for a few minutes. After a few minutes, using a knife, you can cut the stem and root off, and the peel will come off quite easily.

When reading processed food labels, it's not so much the calories that we should count and worry about.
It's the chemicals and the sugar amount.
Question the overall nourishment and whether that product is lifeless and energy draining.

Serves: 4-6
Prep Time: about 40 min.
Marinating Time: several hours or overnight
Cooking Time: 1 hour of baking or 20 minutes of grilling

Traditionally cooked in a special clay oven called *tandoor,* this classic East Indian dish is usually served with steamed basmati rice flavoured with saffron, and garnished with raisins and coriander.
Chutney, raita and the famous flatbread *naan* are other typical accompaniments.
Very few people have a *tandoor* in their kitchen or backyard;
however, we still can achieve great results cooking the chicken using our oven or barbecue.
The chicken is often deeply coloured with red food dye while marinating. I prefer not to use any colouring.
It is best to prepare the chicken the day before you plan on serving it.

Chicken:

3 lbs of chicken thighs, skinless,
washed and patted dry
1 tbsp salt dissolved in the juice of 1 lemon

Marinade:

1 tsp vegetable oil
2 tsp coriander seeds
1 tsp cumin seeds
5 cloves
1 tsp black peppercorns
¾ cup plain yogurt
1 tsp ground turmeric
½ tsp hot pepper flakes
2 garlic cloves, peeled
1 small onion, peeled
1 tbsp fresh ginger, chopped

Celtic salt
To garnish: fresh coriander leaves,
lime and tomato wedges

Fresh Mango Chutney:

Combine all ingredients in a bowl.
Macerate for 2 hours in the refrigerator.

2 mangoes, not quite ripe, peeled, pitted and chopped
2 small hot peppers, seeded and minced
1½ tbsp fresh coriander, finely chopped

½ tsp each of cayenne pepper and curry powder
1 tsp Celtic salt
2 tsp lemon juice

Raita:

Combine all ingredients in a bowl and chill.

1½ cups plain yogurt
1 cup grated cucumber
¼ cup fresh coriander, chopped

½ tsp ground cumin
½ tsp Celtic salt

The day before:

1. Place the chicken pieces in a bowl. Rub the chicken with the salt-lemon mixture. Cover and brine in the refrigerator for 1 hour.
2. **For the marinade:** In a frying pan, heat the oil over medium heat; add the coriander, cumin and cloves, and roast for 1 minute. Transfer these spices and the peppercorns to a blender and pulverize. Add yogurt, turmeric, pepper flakes, garlic, onion, ginger and a pinch of salt. Blend until creamy. Pour the yogurt mixture in a shallow glass dish.
3. Remove the brined chicken from the refrigerator and transfer to the yogurt mixture, coating all pieces very well. Cover; place the dish in the refrigerator. Macerate for several hours or overnight, turning the chicken pieces over several times.

The day of cooking:

a. **If you are baking the chicken**, preheat the oven to 350°F. Place the pieces in a single layer in a large baking dish or roasting pan, ensuring that all the pieces are well coated with the yogurt marinade. Cook for about 1 hour or until crisp and brown. Transfer to a serving platter; garnish with coriander and serve with lime and tomato wedges. Serve with the cooling East Indian **Raita** and the **Fresh Mango Chutney.**
b. **If you are grilling**, warm up the barbecue. Grill the chicken pieces about 10 minutes on each side. Transfer to a serving platter, garnish with coriander and serve with lime and tomato wedges. Serve with the cooling East Indian **Raita** and the **Fresh Mango Chutney.**

Easy and Simple Roast Turkey

Serves 12-14
Prep Time: 30 min.
Cooking Time: about 2 hours

I rarely cook a turkey because it is too much food for just Philip and me. However, a few years ago, while we were grocery shopping for Christmas, I saw small fresh turkeys at our favourite food store. Since we were going out for a Chinese dinner with his family on Christmas day, I proposed to Philip that we could cook the turkey on Boxing Day and make several dishes with the leftovers. He liked the idea. That night, Southern Ontario experienced a massive ice storm causing hundreds of thousands of homes to lose electricity. Three days later, Christmas Eve, still no power and no light in sight, we escaped to our weekend home where there was power and heat. The next day, bad snowy weather forced us to stay where we were and not join his family for dinner. The turkey became our Christmas dinner, our first for just the two of us. I used the following recipe and it was deliciously memorable.

By choosing a small turkey, and omitting the stuffing, the roasting process is much quicker: about 2 hours! You will have enough meat for a dinner, and leftovers for soups, a salad, and whatever else you like. When you de-bone the cooked turkey, make sure you set aside the bones, the skin, (the giblets, if you don't want to eat them), and some fat for a tasty stock. **You will need** a roasting pan large enough to hold the bird, the giblets, and the vegetables. To ensure that the turkey will be very juicy, allow it to rest for about 1 hour at room temperature before roasting it. This time spent to rest outside of the refrigerator allows the internal temperature of the meat to reach 165°F sooner as it roasts, before the outside of the turkey starts to dry. It also allows the muscle fibers to relax after the long refrigeration period which will result in more tender meat.

A small turkey of about 8-12 lbs (preferably fresh for a tastier meat and to save on defrosting time. If you have a frozen turkey, allow 2½-3 days to thaw in the refrigerator before cooking it.)
olive oil
1 celery stalk cut in half, and each half cut in 3 sticks
1 leek, cleaned, cut in half and each half cut in 3 pieces
Celtic salt and pepper

dried parsley, paprika
5 carrots, peeled, cut into chunks
4 celery stalks, cut into chunks
3 onions, peeled, cut into chunks
8-10 white mushrooms, stems removed, cut in half
1 fresh sprig each of fresh rosemary, sage and parsley
water

1. Preheat the oven to 500°F. Remove the giblets (neck, liver, heart) and set aside. Wash the turkey under running water and pat it dry.
2. In the roasting pan, make a rack with the celery sticks and the leek pieces. Place the turkey on the rack, breast side up. With your hands or a brush, rub some oil all over the bird. Sprinkle salt and pepper, parsley and paprika.
3. Distribute the giblets, carrot, celery, onion, mushroom chunks and the fresh herbs around the bird. Add about 1 cup of water in the bottom of the pan. Transfer the pan in the hot oven.
4. Roast for about 20-30 minutes, or until the top begins to brown; then, turn the heat down to 350°F. Continue to roast, basting with the pan juices every 30 minutes or so. If the top seems to brown too quickly, cover with a piece of foil. Make sure that there is always juice in the bottom of the pan, adding ½ cup of water at a time, when it is necessary.
5. The turkey is done when an instant-read thermometer inserted into the thickest part of the thigh reads 155-165°F. When the turkey is almost done, if the top is not browned enough, increase the heat to 425°F for the last 20-30 minutes of cooking.
6. When cooked, let the turkey rest for 15-20 minutes so its juices, forced to the centre by the heat, are redistributed back into the meat. Transfer it to a serving platter for carving. On a separate platter, transfer the vegetables and giblets, if using. Strain the pan juices. Serve the meat with the vegetables, giblets, and the pan juices. Invite some people over and enjoy this healthy spa food worthy of a celebration.

Note: If you want a gravy-like sauce, purée the strained pan juices with a few pieces of onion, carrot, celery and mushroom that were roasting with the turkey. Season to taste with salt and pepper. Enjoy! This is great food!

Beef and Lamb

Be a food label reader;
choose fresh, basic ingredients over packaged processed food;
cook your own meals more often.

Bœuf bourguignon
(Beef Stew with Red Wine)

Serves 6
Prep Time: 1 hour
Cooking Time: 3 hours

At the end of the summer, when the days are becoming noticeably shorter and cooler,
I always look forward to warming, heavier dishes like this stew.
I think it makes an awesome comfort food with lots of umami (or yummy) taste!
I like this stew with lots of vegetables.

It seems long and complicated to make; however, the result is very much worth the effort. Not only will you have a delicious stew, you will also have a spa-healthy sauce that will keep everything moist. Depending on the number of diners (and their appetite), you may have plenty of leftovers for several meals. Many deliciously rich stews like this one taste even better the next day as the flavours have more time to mingle and marry.

To thicken the juices without using wheat flour, cornstarch or cream,
I create a rich and flavourful gravy-sauce by puréeing the cooked vegetables. I hope you will like it!

Stew recipes like this one need some time to prepare and cook, so you need to book some time to be in the kitchen, like a Sunday afternoon. Please note that once the stew is gently bubbling away in the oven, you will have free time to do other things, like taking a **relaxing bath** with a **facial gommage**, while your house is gradually being filled with the mouth-watering aroma.

3 tbsp olive oil
2 lbs organic beef chuck, cut into 2-inch cubes, or
3 lbs of beef short ribs
12-15 pearl onions, peeled☺
1 lb mushrooms, cleaned, quartered
2 large sweet onions, chopped
1½ cups each of finely chopped carrots and celery
1 large shallot, chopped
2 garlic cloves, minced
Celtic salt and pepper, to taste
½ cup red wine of your choice
(i.e., Burgundy, Pinot Noir, Merlot)
3 cups organic beef broth or more

1 tbsp tomato paste
1 cup canned plum tomatoes, chopped or crushed
2 bay leaves
2 thyme sprigs
2 tbsp rosemary needles, chopped
3 large carrots, peeled, cut into 1-inch pieces
2 large parsnips, peeled, cut into 1-inch pieces
1 celery branch, cut into 1-inch pieces
2-3 large handfuls of green and yellow
string beans, trimmed, and cut in half
1 zucchini, cut in half moons
Chopped parsley, for garnish
1-2 tbsp maple syrup

1. On a plate, pat the beef cubes dry with a paper towel. Season with salt and pepper. Set aside.
2. In a large Dutch oven, heat 1 tbsp olive oil over a medium-high flame. In small batches, brown the beef cubes on all sides. Take your time to do this important step: the deep browning of the meat pieces on the bottom of the pot will create a wonderfully rich and tasty sauce. Remove the browned meat pieces and set aside in a bowl.
3. While you continue browning the beef cubes in the Dutch oven, in a frying pan, heat some oil to cook the pearl onions until golden brown. Set aside in a bowl. Cook the mushroom quarters in the frying pan, stirring often until they have released their moisture, the moisture has evaporated (concentrating the flavour) and they have turned golden brown. Set aside in a bowl. Pour some beef broth in the frying pan to deglaze (to dislodge with your wooden spoon the caramelized and flavourful food bits from the bottom of the pan). Reserve the liquid to be added to the stew later.
4. Back in the Dutch oven, add a bit more oil. Add the chopped onions and cook until golden. Add the chopped carrots and celery and cook until softened, about 10-15 minutes. Add the shallot and garlic. Cook for a few minutes. Season with salt and pepper.
5. Pour in the wine, stir and let the alcohol evaporate for a few minutes, while you scrape the bottom of the Dutch oven with your spoon to dislodge caramelized, flavourful food bits.
6. Pour in the beef broth and the tomato paste; cook for 10-15 minutes (or more) until the vegetables are soft. Once the vegetables are soft, add the reserved liquid from the pearl onions and mushrooms, and the tomatoes and, with a hand-held immersion blender (or a potato masher, which will give you a coarser texture), purée the mixture to obtain a more or less smooth consistency. That will be your **gravy-sauce**.
7. Preheat the oven to 325°F. Return the beef cubes to the Dutch oven. Add the bay leaves, the thyme branches, the rosemary, the carrot, the celery, and the parsnip pieces. Add more beef broth to cover the meat and vegetables, if necessary; stir and adjust the seasoning, if you feel it is needed.
8. Bring the content of the Dutch oven to a boil. Cover with a lid and place in the oven to cook for about 2 hours. During this slow-and-low cooking (slow-cooking at low-heat) that will break up the beef cubes into soft and succulent easily-pulled-apart fibers, you may check periodically the level of "doneness" of the meat.
9. After 2 hours of cooking, add the pearl onions, the mushrooms, the green and yellow beans, and the zucchini to the stew. Cook for another 45 minutes or so, until the meat fibers can easily be pulled apart, and the hard vegetables are tender. Remove from the oven.
10. Check the seasoning again. If the tomatoes have made the sauce a little too acidic, add 1-2 tbsp of maple syrup to balance the flavours. Remove the bay leaves and what is left of the thyme sprigs.
11. To serve, I like to remove the bones and the membranes, and break up the bigger pieces of meat so what the guests will find in their bowls is a ready-to-eat stew consisting of tender meat fibers, soft vegetables and a rich, unctuous sauce. Serve this stew over creamy mashed potatoes and a side dish of green salad and you will have a GREAT dinner worthy of "*Mmmm! This is sooo good!*" from your happy diners.

☺To peel the pearl onions more easily (and without any tears!), soak them in a bowl of very hot water for a few minutes. After a few minutes, using a knife, you can cut the stem and root off, and the peel will come off quite easily.

Variations:

In step 7, you can add:

- 4 strips of zest from 1 orange, removed with a vegetable peeler, each strip about 3 inches long, cleaned of pith.
- If you like olives, ½ cup of well drained pitted olives to be cooked with the stew; and another ½ cup before serving to maximize their impact.

Things that feel like a mini vacation to me:
Sitting outdoors in the sun, listening and observing;
A walk in nature whether at the beach, in the park, near flowing water, or anywhere I can see lots of greenery and the blue sky;
Watching the sun rise and set;
Having some time to read a book I have been craving to devour;
Enjoying a cup of tea and a chat with a close friend or a loved one;
Playing a board game with fun-loving participants;
Working on a creative project that I truly enjoy;
Dancing and singing with music that moves me;
RESTING: to recharge, to "resource" myself.

What feels like a mini vacation for you?

Agneau à l'orange
(Lamb with Fresh Oranges)

Serves 4
Prep Time: 15 min.
Cooking Time: about 2 hours

It is the **bouquet garni** consisting of herbs and a piece of dried orange peel that makes this rustic Southern France stew quite aromatic. If you don't care for lamb, beef works well, too.

2 lbs of lamb, cut in 1½-inch cubes, seasoned with Celtic salt and pepper
2 tbsp olive oil
2 onions, quartered
2 carrots, cut in chunks
1 cup of dry white wine
1 cup of beef or chicken stock
A bouquet garni☺

1 garlic clove, minced
Celtic salt and pepper
1 tbsp maple syrup
2-3 tbsp freshly squeezed orange juice
1 tsp hot pepper flakes
The segments of 1 peeled orange
Chopped parsley to garnish

1. In a Dutch oven, heat the oil over medium heat. Brown the meat cubes on all sides, turning them often. When they are browned, transfer them to a bowl and set aside.
2. Add more oil if needed. Cook the onions and carrots for 15 minutes or so, stirring until the onions are golden brown and soft. Preheat the oven to 325°F.
3. Add the wine and bring to a boil while stirring. Reduce the heat and add the stock, the bouquet garni and the garlic. Return the meat cubes to the Dutch oven, cover and transfer to the oven to simmer over low heat for 1 hour.
4. After the first cooking hour, heat up the maple syrup in a small saucepan with the orange juice and about ¼ of the cooking liquid, until boiling point. Add this sweet liquid to the Dutch oven and continue cooking, covered, for an additional 45 minutes or more, until the lamb cubes are fork-tender and the meat fibers easily separate.

5. Transfer the lamb to a side dish, cover to keep warm. Strain the cooking liquid into a saucepan, pressing on the vegetables with a spoon to release their juices and create a thick gravy-sauce. Return the squashed vegetables to the Dutch oven. Bring the gravy-sauce in the saucepan to a boil, reduce the heat and simmer for 15 minutes.
6. Skim the fat that you see on the surface of the sauce. Taste and adjust the seasoning, if needed. Pour the sauce in the Dutch oven and add the meat. Add the pepper flakes and the orange segments, and allow to heat through. Serve hot in bowls garnished with the chopped parsley.

☺**Bouquet garni:** a piece of **dried orange peel***; 1 **bay leaf**; a few sprigs of fresh **parsley** and **thyme**; a few **celery leaves** (or lovage, if you have any). Wrap all ingredients in a square of cheese cloth and tie with a piece of kitchen string.

Moroccan Lamb with Potatoes and Olives

Serves 4
Prep Time: 10 min.
Marinating Time: 2 hours or overnight
Cooking Time: 1¾ hours

A comforting winter dish that can be served with the **Moroccan Blood Oranges and Beets Salad** from the **Loading Up on the Greens** section.

1 lb lamb, or beef, cut into cubes

Marinade:

1 small sweet onion, grated
3 tbsp olive oil
3 tbsp each of parsley and coriander, finely chopped
1 garlic clove, minced

½ tsp cumin seeds
½ tsp each of ground ginger and ground coriander
Celtic salt
Fresh parsley and coriander, chopped

Water
Celtic salt
⅓ cup green olives (not the stuffed variety)

Pinch of saffron
3 potatoes, peeled and cut into medium chunks
To garnish: freshly chopped parsley and coriander

1. Add the meat cubes to the marinade in a Ziploc bag. Seal and toss the meat cubes to evenly coat in the marinade. Marinate for at least 2 hours on the kitchen counter, or overnight in the refrigerator.
2. Transfer the meat and the marinade to a saucepan. Add 3 cups of water, 1 tsp salt and bring to a boil. Cover and simmer for 1½ hours.
3. Add the olives and continue to simmer for another 15 minutes.
4. In another saucepan, add 3 cups of water and bring to a boil. Add the saffron, 2 tsp of salt, and the potatoes. Simmer until they are tender, about 20 minutes. Drain.
5. Transfer the cooked meat cubes to a serving platter, cover to keep warm. If there is still some cooking liquid in the saucepan, bring it to a boil to reduce it to a thicker sauce. Pour it over the meat cubes.
6. Place the potatoes around the meat, and sprinkle with the chopped herbs.

* When you peel oranges, save the peels on a plate and let them dry uncovered for a few days. When they are dry, store them in a glass jar to have on hand for soups, stews, desserts, etc.

Serves 4-6
Prep Time: 10-15 min.
Cooking Time: 10-15 min.

These lovely meat cakes can also be made with ground turkey or ground lamb.
You can add a small cube of cheese, like Jarlsberg or Emmenthal, inside the centre of each of the uncooked meat cakes. As an interesting condiment, you can top the cakes with the **Mango and Avocado Salsa** below or the **Melon Salsa** found in the **Loading Up on the Greens** chapter.

¼ cup ground flaxseeds	¼ cup sun-dried tomatoes, chopped
¼ cup hemp seeds	1 lb lean ground beef
¼ cup coconut flour	Celtic salt and pepper to taste
2 tbsp each fresh parsley and basil, finely chopped	½ apple or pear, grated
1 tbsp chives, finely chopped	Pinch of hot pepper flakes
1 egg, lightly beaten	**To serve:** lettuce leaves
½ cup parmesan, grated (optional)	

1. In a mixing bowl, combine all the ingredients except the lettuce leaves. The best way to incorporate all these ingredients is with your hands, after you "de-bling", of course.
2. Shape into 6-8 cakes and place on a plate. Lightly oil each side of the cakes.
3. Heat up the grill. Grill the cakes until cooked, about 6-8 minutes. Flip them over and cook for another 6-8 minutes, or until the inside is cooked.
4. Remove from the hot grill and place on a clean plate. Cover with a piece of foil for a few minutes. Serve on a bed of green leaves, like arugula.

Variation:

Wrap in a Boston Bibb or romaine lettuce and enjoy as a hamburger with your favourite toppings.

Mango and Avocado Salsa:

Place all ingredients in a medium bowl.
Gently toss to combine and refrigerate, covered, for 30 minutes before serving.

1 medium mango, peeled, pitted and coarsely chopped	1 fresh small red thai chili, finely chopped
1 large avocado, coarsely chopped	2 tbsp lime juice
1 small red onion, finely chopped	
1 small red pepper, finely chopped	

Serves 3-4
Prep Time: 20-30 min.
Cooking Time: 8-10 min.

While walking the periphery of a European or Asian grocery store, I often get inspiration for a meal. The following simple recipe was created one day as I explored the produce aisle of one of my favorite grocery stores and gathered fresh ingredients that appealed to me. Creative inspiration for a healthy and toothsome meal often comes when you are a bit hungry. But not too hungry, because it is very easy to succumb to ripping open a bag of not-so-good carbs and scarfing down most of its content. Use this recipe as a canvas to create your own impromptu meal with fresh and colourful ingredients that you already have at home or that you will find at

the grocery store during your next visit. Use your imagination and be bold. If you are pleased with your creation, make sure you record the ingredients and how you did it. I know it will be wonderful!

Lamb Chops:

1-2 packages of fresh New Zealand spring lamb
chops (or pork chops or beef steaks)
Celtic salt and pepper
Fresh rosemary sprigs, chopped
Coconut oil or butter

Season the chops with salt, pepper and rosemary. Heat the oil or butter in a pan and cook the chops over medium-hot heat a few minutes on each side, until they are cooked to your liking. Set aside, covered with a piece of foil until serving time.

Salad:

1 head of Romaine lettuce and other lettuce leaves
1 cup of fresh pitted olives of your choice
6-8 sun-dried tomatoes in oil, cut in thin slivers
¼ of a red onion, thinly sliced
1 mini cucumber, sliced

1 small orange pepper, seeded and sliced
A few artichoke hearts in oil
Fresh parsley and rosemary, chopped
Celtic salt and pepper

Divide and arrange the ingredients on serving plates.

Vinaigrette:

Put the following ingredients in a screw-top glass jar. Screw the lid on and shake vigorously to combine. Drizzle over the salad.

2 tbsp extra virgin olive oil
2 tbsp balsamic vinegar (or other vinegar)
1 tsp Dijon mustard

1 tsp honey
Celtic salt and pepper

Did you know that storing tomatoes in the refrigerator will diminish their flavour?
They will keep longer and have more flavour if they are stored at room temperature stem side down.

Serves 4
Prep Time: 20 min.
Cooking Time: about 3 hours

A wonderful family dish of "low-and-slow" cooked meat and vegetables that is sure to make your guests smile and ask for more. This type of comforting spa "slow food" (*vs.* fast food) is well worth the effort. Depending on the size of the appetite of your guests, you should have leftovers for a few extra meals. In my family, we add marrow bones for extra flavour and nutrients. Marrow bones provide delicious gelatin to the broth which gives it more body. When cooked, the rich, buttery marrow can easily be removed from the hollow of the bone with a knife, and then spread on gluten-free crackers or toasts. Add some freshly chopped parsley, salt and pepper, and you have a lovely treat!

Bouquet Garni:

Wrap in a cheese cloth the following herbs. Tie with a kitchen twine and set aside.
2 bay leaves, 8 black peppercorns, 2 sprigs of thyme, 3-4 sprigs of parsley

Pot-au-feu:

1 blade roast of about 3 lb (or any other inexpensive cuts of meat, like bone-in beef short ribs, that require "low and slow" cooking to break down the tough meat fiber and melt the collagen into a tender and delicious meat stew)
Optional: About 2 lb beef marrow bones, rinsed and sprinkled with salt and pepper.
1 sweet onion, peeled, quartered
1 celery stalk, cut into chunks
3 carrots, peeled, cut into chunks

2 parsnips, peeled, centre core removed, cut into chunks
½ of a small cabbage, cut into 8 wedges
½ lb each of green beans and yellow wax beans, trimmed and cut in half
1 zucchini, cut into chunks
Celtic salt and pepper to taste
A handful of fresh parsley, chopped
8 small red potatoes, scrubbed. To keep the broth clear, it is best to boil the potatoes separately in salted water for 15-20 minutes and drain.

Flavour Enhancers:

Arrange the following condiments in separate serving bowls.

Salt and pepper
Gluten-free horseradish
Grainy mustard

Cornichons or sweet pickles
Olives

1. In a large Dutch oven, put the piece(s) of meat and the onion. Pour enough water to cover. Add the bouquet garni. Heat over medium heat and bring to a gentle boil. Skim the surface if necessary. Reduce the heat to the lowest setting. Cover and simmer until meat is tender, about 2 hours. During this time, you are free to go do something else! So, go!
2. After 2 hours, increase the heat to high and let the meat and vegetables come to a boil. Add marrow bones (if using), celery and carrots, parsnips, and cabbage. Add more water if needed to cover the vegetables.
3. Reduce the heat to simmer and cover. Cook until vegetables are almost fork tender, about 15 to 20 minutes.
4. Add the beans and zucchini, cover and cook until the beans are tender crisp, and the carrots and parsnips are fork tender. Add the cooked potatoes to warm them up.
5. Transfer the vegetables, the meat and the marrow bones to a large serving platter. Cover with foil to keep warm. Remove the bouquet garni. Reduce the broth over high heat. Taste it and adjust the seasoning if needed. Pour it in a measuring cup.
6. Slice the meat. Ladle some broth over the meat and the vegetables. Garnish the serving platter with chopped parsley. Serve the meat and the vegetables with the broth and the **flavour enhancers**.

Swimming Protein with Scales and Shells

Fish and Seafood

I find fresh fish and seafood the easiest food to prepare because not much is required to bring out their delicate flavour, sweetness, juicy-ness, and tender texture. Steaming, pan-frying, baking, grilling or poaching are often the quickest and most effective methods of cooking fish and seafood to guarantee the best flavours and keep their glistening textures intact. Just a few minutes of cooking and basic flavouring – such as citrus juice and zest, herbs, spices, oil, some vegetables, and even fruits – are all that is required to make a fish or seafood dish simple but outstanding in flavours.

Whenever possible, for optimal taste and quality, when you shop at your favourite fish store, request fish and seafood fresh from the sea instead of a fish farm where they may have been fed antibiotics and other offensively toxic agents.

(Pictured below is my favourite spot by the beach in "The Feel Good Town" of Cobourg.)

No-fuss Baked Fish Dinner with Mango Salsa

Serves 4
Prep Time: 10 min.
Cooking Time: 20-25 min.

This is a quick and simple dinner when time is a rare commodity and inspired creativity to whip up something different is running low. Use whatever fresh pieces of fish you can find and be careful not to over-cook them. I like salmon fillet or sea bass. Served with steamed vegetables and a green salad prepared while the fish is baking, this is a great, simple, flavourful spa weeknight dinner. Or any night dinner. If you don't have time to prepare the salsa, don't worry; do it another time.

A fish fillet big enough for 4 persons
Vegetable oil
Juice of ½ lemon, ¼ orange, ½ lime (or a combination)
Zest of ½ lemon, ½ orange, ½ lime (or a combination)

Celtic salt and pepper to taste
Hot red pepper or piment d'Espelette
1 tsp fresh dill, chopped, or ½ tsp dried dill

1. Wash the fish, flesh and skin, well. With your fingers, feel the flesh for any bones. If you find some, remove them with tweezers (I have tweezers that I keep only as a kitchen tool). Let the fish dry for a few minutes on paper towel, flesh down.
2. Lightly oil the centre of a foil-lined baking sheet where you will put the fish. Preheat the oven to 350°F.
3. Place the fish fillet skin down on the oiled baking sheet. Drizzle the citrus juice(s) over the flesh. Sprinkle the zest over the flesh, season with salt and pepper, hot red pepper, and dill.
4. Bake for about 20 minutes, depending on the thickness of the slices or fillets. With a fork, check for doneness by lifting the top layer of flesh in the centre of the fish. Flaky? It is done. Still a bit raw? Keep cooking for a few more minutes.
5. To serve, with a spatula, cut a section of the fish; then, slide the spatula between the flesh and the skin and lift the fish onto a serving plate.

Salsa:

1 large mango, cut into thin strips
½ cucumber, seeded and cut into thin strips
1-2 green onions, sliced
3 tbsp lime juice

1 tbsp coriander, chopped
1 small jalapeño pepper, seeded, finely chopped
1 garlic clove, minced

In a medium bowl, combine all the ingredients. Cover and chill until ready to use.
Instead of mango, other fruit can be used like pineapple or peaches.

Do you know the meaning of 'we're in a kettle of fish'?
We're in an awful mess.

Aromatic Thai Seafood Stew

Serves: 4
Prep Time: 25 min.
Cooking Time: 10 min.

This special dish calls for a celebratory occasion. Use the freshest seafood that you can find and afford.
Even with just one variety, the stew will be extraordinary. It can be served with a salad and a vegetable side dish.

A- 1½ cups coconut milk (you can use
chicken or fish broth instead)
2 lemongrass stalks, cut into 2-inch pieces
1 tbsp fish sauce
1 tsp galangal, finely grated to a purée (or fresh ginger)
6-8 white mushrooms, quartered or sliced
Juice of 1 lime
½ tsp hot sauce or Sambal Oelek
1 tsp cane sugar or maple syrup
1 large handful of snow peas, trimmed and halved

B- 2 tbsp vegetable oil
12-16 shrimp, peeled, deveined and halved lengthwise
12-16 small scallops, or 8 large ones, halved lengthwise
4-6 oz fish of your choice, cut into bite-size pieces

To garnish: A small handful of fresh coriander leaves
A small handful of Thai basil leaves
or regular basil leaves
Lime wedges

1. In a large pot, put all the ingredients from the **A** section, and gently simmer for 10 minutes, especially if you are using coconut milk as it will separate if brought to the boiling point.
2. When the broth is almost ready, in a skillet, heat the oil. Cook the ingredients from the **B** section for 2-3 minutes until the shrimp are turning pink, and the scallops and fish are opaque.
3. Divide the seafood between serving bowls. Spoon the broth over. Garnish with the fresh herbs and a lime wedge to squeeze over the seafood.

Serves 4
Prep Time: 20 min.
Cooking Time: 16-18 min.

A *papillote* is a French term for a simple cooking method: wrapping foods in packets made of foil, parchment paper, vegetable leaves, or banana leaves, and baking them so the contents gently steam and their juicy flavours marry beautifully. The papillotes can be prepared ahead of time, they contain minimal fat, and they are easy to clean up after the meal. This is a beautiful meal in itself, wrapped like a gift and presented on a plate. The diners wait with excitement to open their surprise. In place of the potato scales, you can rest the fish on other thinly sliced vegetables, like sweet potatoes, zucchini rounds, tomatoes slices, etc. This is the ultimate spa dish!

4 pieces of fresh salmon, about 3-4" by 2", and 1" in thickness, bones and scales removed
1 tbsp olive oil
4 potatoes, peeled and very thinly sliced (with a mandolin, if you have one)
Soft butter or olive oil

3 tbsp chopped parsley
1 garlic clove, minced
Lemon juice
Lemon zest
Fresh or dried dill
Celtic salt, black pepper and red pepper flakes

1. Preheat oven to 350°F. Make 4 papillotes☺ with parchment paper or aluminum foil.
2. Rub a little oil on the inside bottom of each packet so the potato slices will not stick to the paper or foil. Arrange the potato slices like fish scales or roof shingles on 3 rows on each of the packet. Lightly dab them with some butter or rub them with olive oil; season with salt and pepper, parsley, garlic and red pepper flakes.

3. Place a piece of salmon on top of the potato slices in each packet. Drizzle some lemon juice. Lightly season with salt and pepper. Sprinkle the lemon zest and dill over each salmon piece.
4. Close the packet. Transfer to 2 large baking sheets. Bake for 16-18 minutes.*
5. Serve immediately. **Be careful** when you open the papillotes: **the cloud of aromatic steam is very hot**, especially if your face is right above it!

☺**How to make a papillote – a kitchen craft project:**

For each serving, fold in half a 15-inch square piece of parchment paper or aluminum foil. Open the paper like you would a book. Place the ingredients on one half of the paper near the crease. When ready to close the packet, bring the "cover" (the empty side) over the ingredients, aligning the edges together. To seal the packet, make tight overlapping folds along the edges. I often staple the edges so the fragrant steam doesn't escape during cooking.

> *"As you walk and eat and travel, be where you are.*
> *Otherwise you will miss most of your life."*
> -Buddha

---

* Near the end of the cooking time, I open one packet to check if the salmon and the potatoes are cooked to the consistency I like. If they are not quite cooked, I close the packet as best as I can and return it in the oven with the other 3 to cook a little further. That packet will be mine at the time of serving. I like to serve the unopened papillotes on a plate and let the guests open theirs in the middle with a pair of scissors, after I warn them to be mindful of the hot steam.

Visit my website at www.olivestolychees.com for a demonstration.

Serves 4-6
Prep Time: 20 min.
Cooking Time: 15-20 min.

You choose how you want to enjoy this seafood dish: as an appetizer, an entrée, or a soup. You can serve it with **Asian Grain-free Crackers** or toasted slices of the **Four-herb Wonder Bread,** both recipes from the **Wholesome and Nourishing Baking** section. When serving, have an empty bowl handy for the discarded empty shells.

2 tbsp olive or vegetable oil
I large onion, finely chopped
1 shallot, finely chopped
1 large carrot, finely chopped
2 celery stalks, finely chopped
½ red pepper, finely chopped
½ green pepper, finely chopped
1 garlic clove, finely chopped
1 tbsp ginger, finely chopped
1 lemongrass stem, chopped in 2-inch pieces
3-4 kaffir lime leaves
4-5 tomatoes, cored and chopped
(or 1½ cups canned diced tomatoes)

½ cup Riesling wine
3-4 cups chicken broth (or fish stock,
if you happen to have some on hand)
1 tbsp fish sauce
1-2 tbsp organic tamari
2-3 tsp Thai curry paste☺
A squirt of chili oil or 1 tsp Sambal Oelek

4 lbs mussels, cleaned and de-bearded
A handful of fresh basil leaves, cut
in thin ribbons with scissors
A handful of fresh coriander, chopped

1. In a large pot, heat the oil over medium heat. Add the onion and shallot; cook until the onion is translucent. Add the carrot, celery, peppers, garlic, ginger, lemongrass, and kaffir lime leaves. Cook for a few minutes until fragrant.
2. Add the tomatoes and cook for 1-2 minutes. Add the wine and bring to a boil. Pour in the chicken broth, the fish sauce, the tamari, the curry paste and the chili oil or Sambal Oelek. Bring the liquids back to a boil.
3. Add the mussels, bring back to a boil; then, lower the heat to simmer, and cover. Let the mussels cook for a few minutes until they open. Taste the broth and adjust the seasoning, if necessary.
4. Discard any mussel that doesn't open. Discard the kaffir lime leaves and the lemongrass pieces as they have fulfilled their flavouring purpose. Add the herbs and toss to combine.
5. Fill individual bowls with the mussels and pour the fragrant broth over. Serve hot.

☺Thai curry paste is available in jars in Asian food stores and many grocery stores. There are different kinds. You may want to try a few and see which one(s) you prefer.

Variation:

If you want to serve this dish as a soup, you can remove all the mussel meat from the shells, and discard the empty shells prior to serving.

Satisfying the Sweet Tooth

Desserts

There are special occasions that require decadent desserts, and, without a beautiful mouth-watering dessert, the celebration wouldn't be complete. Desserts are fun to make and even more fun to eat. After all, desserts make people very happy!

In moderation, the healthier fruit-based, flavoured spa indulgences in this chapter will satisfy you without making you feel guilty, remorseful, or ill afterwards. Or having to run a 10K marathon to burn off the excess calories! By focusing on key flavourful ingredients -- fruits, nuts, spices, chocolate, vanilla, etc – as the shining stars of the dessert, you will notice that quality and taste are not sacrificed. And you won't miss the sugar. Enjoy and feel good!

1 – Vibrant Fruit Desserts

Indian Broiled Mango

Serves 2
Prep Time: 5 min.
Broiling Time: 10 min.

Broiling brings out the sweetness of the mango, which contrasts very well with the tartness of the lime. The cardamom adds an interesting dimension.

1 mango, peeled and sliced
1 lime, zested and juiced

Ground cardamom
To garnish: fresh mint leaves

1. Preheat the broiler to 500°F.
2. Arrange the mango slices in a single layer on a broiler pan covered with foil.
3. Broil 8-10 minutes until browned in some spots.
4. Remove from oven. Place on a serving plate. Squeeze lime juice over the mango slices. Sprinkle the zest and some cardamom. Garnish with mint leaves.

Broiled Stone Fruits

Serves 4
Prep Time: 10 min.
Broiling Time: 4-6 min.

Broiling caramelizes these sugar-dusted fruits and elevates this simple dessert to a fancy level.
After a copious meal, this bright and fresh finish will leave you satisfied without feeling that you have overindulged.

2 peaches, stones removed and cut into slices
2 plums, stones removed and cut into slices
2 nectarines, stones removed and cut into slices

1 orange, peeled, and pith removed, sliced or segmented
1 tbsp cane or coconut sugar

1. Heat broiler. Divide the fruits among 4 shallow ovenproof ramekins.
2. Sprinkle with sugar. Transfer ramekins to a rimmed baking sheet.
3. Broil, rotating the baking sheet once, until the fruits are golden brown, 4-6 minutes.

Variations:

- You can add ground spices like cinnamon, clove and ginger before broiling.
- A spoonful of vanilla-scented whipped cream or plain Greek yogurt would make this dessert *seem* decadent.
- For a delicate herbal quality, top the fruits with finely cut lemon verbena or mint leaves.

Thai Lychees and Lemongrass

Serves 4
Prep Time: 10 min.
Optional Cooking Time: 10 min.

Simple, quick and refreshing, that is what this dessert is about. Serve in glasses or small bowls.
You can also use fresh longans when they are available at the Asian markets.

Using Fresh Lychees:

24 fresh lychees, peeled and seeded
2 pieces of candied ginger, finely chopped

Finely grated zest and juice of 1 lime
1 starfruit (or carambola)

1. In a mixing bowl, combine lychees, candied ginger, lime zest and juice.
2. Distribute in 4 glasses or bowls.
3. With a vegetable peeler, remove the brown edges of the starfruit. Using a mandolin, slice the starfruit very thinly crosswise. Decorate the glasses with 2 "stars".

Using Canned Lychees:

1 16-oz can of lychees, drained. Reserve the syrup.
1 piece of gingerroot of 1 inch, peeled and grated
1 stalk of lemongrass cut in 3-4 pieces and smashed

1. In a saucepan, combine the lychee syrup, the grated ginger and the lemongrass. Bring to a boil for about 10 minutes, until thickened. Remove from the heat and let cool.
2. When ready to serve, strain the syrup. Distribute evenly the lychees in 4 glasses or bowls. Pour some of the syrup over the lychees.
3. Finish the dessert with Step 3 as described above.

If you can't think straight, take a nap!

Serves 4
Prep Time: 15 min.
Cooking Time: 15 min.

To create new versions of this simple dessert, experiment with various combinations of ripe stone fruits and spice blends.

3 tbsp butter
3 tbsp honey or less
4 ripe nectarines, halved and pitted
Zest of an orange and 2 tbsp orange juice
½ tsp each of cinnamon, ginger, cloves
1 star anise
Pinch of nutmeg

Optional: 1 cup of heavy cream☺ or plain yogurt whipped with 1 tsp of maple syrup and 1 tsp vanilla

1. In a cast-iron or regular non-stick skillet, melt butter over medium-high heat. When the butter is melted, stir in the honey.
2. Place the nectarine halves, cut side down, in the hot butter-honey mixture. Reduce the heat to medium; cook for about 5 minutes or until the cut sides begin to golden and the nectarine flesh softens. The honey will start to bubble and expand.
3. Reduce the heat to low. Add orange zest, juice, and spices. Stir to distribute evenly.
4. Gently turn nectarines over and cook for a few more minutes.
5. On each serving plate, place 2 nectarine halves and spoon the spicy buttery syrup over. If desired, top each serving with a small dollop of whipped cream. Serve immediately.

☺For different flavouring ideas, you might want to refer to the **Flavoured Whipped Cream** recipe found in the **Part 1 – Vibrant Fruit Desserts** section of **Volume 1.**

Spicy Pineapple

Serves 4-6
Prep Time: 10-15 min.
Cooking Time: 15-20 min.

You will like this exotic dessert: the fragrances and the flavours are addictive. You might want to lick the pan!

1 tbsp unsalted butter or coconut oil
1 tbsp sucanat or maple syrup
1 tsp vanilla
1 pineapple, peeled and cut into ½-inch cubes
1 tsp each of ground cinnamon
1 star anise
1 pinch of saffron
To garnish: 4-6 cinnamon sticks, 4-6 star anise

In a pan, melt the butter; then, add the sweetener and vanilla. Add the pineapple cubes and toss to caramelize for a few minutes. Add the ground cinnamon and the star anise. Cover and cook for 10 minutes over low heat. Remove from the heat. Sprinkle the saffron over the pineapple. Serve in glasses, and garnish with a cinnamon stick and a star anise.

- Instead of the vanilla, cinnamon, star anise, and saffron, you can use ground ginger and ½ tsp chili powder.
- Instead of caramelizing the pineapple cubes in the pan, broil them in the oven for about 3 minutes with the ginger and chili powder.

Mango Orange and Lime Ice

Makes 6 cups
Prep Time: about 25 min.
Freezing Time: 8 hours

A luscious mango purée with a tangy flavour that is fairly quick to prepare;
you just have to be patient for the freezer to do its magic.

2 lbs very ripe mangoes, peeled and pitted
Pinch of Celtic salt
Thin strips of lime zest, made with a zester

1 tsp lime juice
Thin strips of orange zest, made with a zester
1 tsp orange juice

1. Cut the mango flesh in chunks. Line a cookie sheet with a piece of plastic wrap, and spread the chunks in a single layer. Freeze mango chunks until hard, for at least 8 hours. (If you are not using them right away, the frozen chunks can be transferred to a freezer bag. In the freezer, they will keep for 1-2 months.)
2. Remove mango chunks from freezer and let soften slightly at room temperature for about 15 minutes.
3. Place chunks in a food processor with the salt. Purée until smooth, about 2 minutes, stopping to scrape the sides of the bowl as needed. Pulse in the lime and orange juices.
4. Serve immediately in pretty bowls; garnish with the lime zest and the orange zest.

When receiving a therapeutic session or enjoying a meal or taking part in a conversation,
it is when we pause, reflect and integrate that magical 'aha' moments happen.

Japanese Lychee and Strawberry Salad

Makes 4-6 cups
Prep Time: 10 minutes

This very easy dessert can be prepared with fresh lychees when they are available. They will need to be peeled and stoned.

1 can lychees in light syrup (if you can't find fresh ones)
2-3 cups of fresh strawberries, washed and hulled
2-3 sprigs of fresh mint
½ tsp matcha powder
Optional: 1 cup of fresh blueberries

1. Drain the lychees, reserving about ¼ cup of the syrup. Cut the lychees in halves or in quarters. Place in a serving bowl.
2. Cut the strawberries in halves or in quarters, the same size as the lychees. Place in the serving bowl. Add the blueberries, if using.
3. Over the fruits, cut the mint leaves in thin ribbons with a pair of scissors.
4. Drizzle the reserved syrup over the fruit salad. Sprinkle the matcha. Gently toss the salad. Chill until serving time.

Makes 20
Prep Time: 15-20 min.
Cooking Time: 5-10 min.

This beautiful and colourful fruit dessert is always a crowd pleaser. No skill required. No baking either! All you need are some good-quality chocolate and large fresh strawberries. This dessert should be made shortly before you plan on serving it, as condensation drops may collect on the chocolate if the strawberries are stored in the refrigerator for more than 1 hour.

8 oz dark chocolate (You can also use semisweet chocolate if you prefer a little more sweetness or if the strawberries are not very sweet.)

1 lb of large strawberries (about 20), washed and dried well. Leave the stems on.
⅓ cup pistachios, finely chopped (optional)

1. Line a baking sheet with parchment or waxed paper. Set aside.
2. Finely chop the chocolate. Place it in a bowl set over (not in) a saucepan of **simmering** water. Stir occasionally, until melted, about 3-5 minutes. Remove from heat.
3. One at a time, dip each strawberry in the melted chocolate, twirling to coat at least half of the strawberry. Remove from the chocolate bowl. If using the pistachios, sprinkle some on the chocolate-covered portion of the strawberry; then, place on the parchment paper. Chill the strawberries for at least 15 minutes to set the chocolate.

Variations:

- You can use melted white chocolate instead of the dark version. Or, for a greater "Wow" effect, drizzle some melted white chocolate over the dark chocolate coating in Step 3, before sprinkling the pistachios.
- You can use other chopped nuts to add a different crunch.

Red Grapefruit and Pomegranate Salad

Serves 4
Prep Time: 5-10 min.
Cooking Time: 5 min.
Chilling Time: 15 min.

Very fragrant and refreshing, this fresh fruit salad is wonderful when you want a light dessert after a copious meal. The rose water fragrance gives this salad an exotic tone.

4 red grapefruits, peeled and
cut into skinless segments or suprêmes
Seeds from 1 pomegranate
1-2 tbsp honey
1 tsp rose water
Ground cinnamon
4 5 fresh mint leaves, finely cut with scissors

In a small saucepan, warm the honey in 4 tbsp of water. Allow to cool for about15 minutes. Add the rose water. To serve, on a platter or individual plates, arrange each grapefruit segment around the platter, pointing to the centre. Sprinkle the pomegranate seeds over the segments. Drizzle the honey sauce over the salad, sprinkle with some cinnamon, and scatter the mint leaves.

Serves 2-4
Prep Time: 10-15 min.
Chilling Time: 1-2 hours

You might want to double this recipe… or not share the salad.

Matcha, a superfood, is a fine powered green tea that plays a prominent role in the history of tea culture. It is green tea leaves (full of chlorophyll) that have been carefully grown under diffused sunlight for 20-30 days before they are harvested, steamed, dried, and then stone-ground into a fine powder. It contains the highest known concentration of antioxidants in a food source. It is considered one of the superfoods for its health benefits.

2 ripe mangoes, peeled and cut in ½-inch slices or ¾" cubes	½ cup pomegranate seeds
	3 sprigs of fresh mint
18 lychees, from a can in a light syrup; reserve the syrup	1 tbsp matcha
2 tbsp rose water	

1. Place the mango slices or cubes in a medium-size bowl.
2. Add the lychees to the mango bowl. Combine the syrup with the rose water and pour over the fruits.
3. Cut half of the mint leaves thinly with scissors. Add to the fruits, and gently toss to combine. Chill for a few hours.
4. To serve, gently toss the fruits, divide in small dishes. Garnish with the pomegranate seeds, the reserved whole mint leaves, and sprinkle the matcha powder.

Variations:

- If you happen to find fresh lychees, after you have peeled them and remove their stones, you can sprinkle them with 1-2 tbsp of cane sugar or sucanat to sweeten them a little.
- Adding papaya pieces, pomelo segments and ground cherries (also known as *physalis*) will make this salad even more exotic.
- If you can't find pomegranate, use a few fresh raspberries instead.

Serves 4
Prep Time: 10 min.

Even though this salad is traditionally served as an accompaniment to a main dish, I love to serve is as a light dessert option. It is, in fact, one of my favorite fruit desserts. I know you will like it, too. Easy, simple, even exotic, this dish can be prepared any time of the year. You can also make it as a part of your breakfast. Orange blossom water can be purchased in Middle-Eastern stores and some grocery stores.

4 oranges
1 tbsp cane sugar or sucanat
1-2 tsp ground cinnamon
1-2 tbsp orange blossom water
Juice of an orange

½ cup roasted almonds (whole or slivers)
Fresh mint leaves

1. On a cutting board, cut off both ends of an orange. Stand the orange on one end and, from the top of the orange, cut the peel downward all around the orange. Cut the skinless orange into ¼-inch slices and arrange in a circle on a serving platter. Repeat with the other oranges, overlapping the slices in concentric circles.
2. Sprinkle the cane sugar or sucanat and the cinnamon over the orange slices.
3. Pour the orange blossom water and the orange juice over the slices and let macerate for a few minutes.
4. Sprinkle the roasted almonds and the mint leaves. Serve with mint tea.

Variations:

- Instead of almonds, you can substitute lightly roasted pistachios.
- Sprinkle some 2-3 tbsp of pomegranate seeds over the orange slices.
- Instead of using cane sugar, you can combine 1-2 tbsp of honey with 1 tbsp or more of orange blossom water; drizzle the mixture over the fruit.

Serves 4
Prep Time: 10-15 min.
Cooking Time: ¾ to 1 hour

A wonderfully fragrant custard that you can serve at Thanksgiving and Christmas gatherings.

½ tsp ground cloves
¼ tsp each of ground ginger and ground nutmeg
1 tsp ground cinnamon
Pinch of Celtic salt
1 cup canned pumpkin purée

2 eggs, beaten
¼ cup maple syrup
1 tsp vanilla
1 cup coconut milk
1 tbsp orange zest

1. Preheat the oven to 350°F. In a small bowl, combine the spices and salt together. Set aside.
2. In a medium bowl, combine the pumpkin purée, the eggs, the maple syrup, the vanilla, the coconut milk, and the orange zest. Add the spice mixture and whisk until well combined.

3. Pour the custard into oven-safe ramekins. Place the ramekins in a baking dish. Place the baking dish in the oven. Create a hot water bath by pouring enough very hot water in the baking dish to come up halfway to the top of the ramekins.
4. Bake for 45-60 minutes or until a toothpick inserted in the centre of a custard comes out clean.
5. When the custards are cooked, carefully remove the baking dish from the oven. Transfer the ramekins to a cooling rack. Serve while still warm or chilled.

Variations:

- You can add ½ cup raisins to the batter before baking.
- At serving time, you can top the custards with a light dusting of cinnamon and flaxseeds, followed by a sprinkle of finely grated orange zest.

Chocolate Bark

Makes 20 pieces
Prep Time: 20 min.
Warming up Time: 10 min.
Cooling Time: 30 min.

Because there are very few ingredients required for this easy recipe, you might want to splurge a little and choose the best chocolate you can find. Dark chocolate is great for this recipe for its rich and deep flavour that complements the toasted nuts and the sweet fruits dotting the surface. Furthermore, if you want to make your bark even more interesting, you can opt for a combination of dark chocolate, milk chocolate and white chocolate, provided that they are gluten free. As for the nuts and dried fruit, anything you think of will be delicious because of the salty-sweet contrast that is so addictive. I would suggest, however, that you limit your toppings to a total of 3 so that each flavour has a chance to shine without getting lost in the mix.

This is a great gift idea for the Holiday season or for Valentine's Day!
Actually, do we really need a special occasion to give and enjoy chocolate?

1 lb dark chocolate, chopped
¾ cup toasted whole almonds, coarsely chopped
⅔ cup candied ginger, thinly sliced

1. Line a baking sheet with a piece of parchment paper.
2. Melt chocolate pieces in a heatproof bowl set over a pot of gently simmering water, stirring often until melted and smooth. Stir in ⅓ each of the almonds and the ginger. Pour melted chocolate onto the parchment paper and gently spread with a spoon or a spatula until an even ½-inch thick coat is achieved.
3. Sprinkle the rest of the almonds and candied ginger pieces. Refrigerate until solid, about 20-30 minutes. Break or cut into pieces. Refrigerated in an airtight container, it can keep 1 week – if it doesn't get eaten before!

Variations:

- Nutty options: cashews, pecans, pistachios, pine nuts, hazelnuts, macadamias, etc. They can be toasted or roasted, whole or chopped.
- Fruity options: apricots, cranberries, cherries, raisins, mango, blueberries, ground cherries, etc.
- You can also sprinkle ¼ tsp Fleur de sel or Maldon salt on top.
- For a dark-white chocolate combo, melt the 2 chocolates separately. Proceed with the dark chocolate according to the recipe above. Once ⅓ of the nuts and fruit are added, drizzle with the white melted chocolate. Using a toothpick or a skewer, swirl the chocolates together. Pour the melted chocolate onto the parchment paper and gently spread with a spoon or a spatula until an even ½-inch thick coat is achieved. Sprinkle with the remaining nuts and fruit. Refrigerate to cool, then cut or break in pieces.
- For an unusual non-vegetarian version(!), in Step 3 you could replace the ginger pieces and sprinkle… chopped bacon pieces that have been cooked until crispy and cooled! Don't laugh! That salty-sweet duo is amazing!

Mango Purée

Makes 1 cup
Prep Time: 10 min.

Very quick to prepare and versatile, this purée is a great topping for ice cream, pancakes, cakes, fruit salad, even grilled chicken. It can be made up to 2 days before serving. Keep refrigerated.

1 ripe mango, peeled, chopped
½-inch piece of gingerroot, peeled, finely grated. Reserve the juice and discard the fibers.
Zest and juice from 1 lime
1 tbsp sucanat, cane sugar or maple syrup
1 tbsp water or so

In a blender, purée the mango pieces and the ginger juice until smooth. Stir in the lime juice and zest, the sweetener and the water. Blend once more, adding more water if the mixture is too thick.

Apple Crisp

Serves 6-8
Prep Time: 15-20 min.
Cooking Time: 30 min.

It is a great autumn dessert when just out of the oven and the smell of cinnamon floats throughout the whole house! It is also delicious with pears and walnuts.

Filling:

6 cups apples, peeled, cored, thinly sliced
Zest and juice of 1 lemon
3-4 tbsp cane or coconut sugar
1 tsp cinnamon
½ cup pine nuts, roasted

Topping:

1 cup blanched almond flour
3-4 tbsp flaxseeds
Pinch of Celtic salt
2 tbsp cane or coconut sugar
½ tsp each of ground cinnamon, allspice and cloves
¼ cup melted butter
1 tsp vanilla

1. Preheat oven to 350°F. Butter the sides and bottom of a baking dish 8" x 8" (20 cm x 20 cm).
2. **Filling:** In a large bowl, combine the filling ingredients, except the pine nuts. Distribute in the buttered baking dish. Sprinkle the pine nuts.
3. **Topping:** In a bowl, combine the almond flour, flaxseeds, salt, sugar and spices. In a separate bowl, combine melted butter and vanilla. Stir the wet ingredients into the dry ingredients; you will obtain a crumbly mixture. Sprinkle the topping mixture over the apples.
4. Bake until the topping is golden, and the apples are cooked and very fragrant, about 30 minutes.

Serves 4
Prep Time: 20 min.
Cooking Time: 3 min.
Chilling Time: 3-4 hours

Easy and delicious, this bright red dessert
is a must during strawberry season.

1½ lbs fresh strawberries
½ cup cane sugar
1 tbsp each of lemon juice and orange juice
Orange zest
Fresh mint leaves, chopped
½ tsp vanilla

2 envelopes (¼ oz each) unflavoured gelatine
Optional: vanilla-flavoured whipped cream

1. Hull and quarter 1 lb of the strawberries. Combine in a medium bowl with sugar, citrus juices, orange zest, mint and vanilla. Set aside, stirring occasionally, about 10 minutes.
2. Place 1 cup of cold water in a small saucepan; sprinkle the gelatine over water. Let stand 5 minutes to soften.
3. Working in batches, purée the strawberry mixture in a blender. If necessary, add enough water to the mixture to measure a total of 3 cups of liquid. Transfer back into the medium bowl, and set aside.
4. Heat softened gelatine over medium heat, just until it begins to bubble around the edges and gelatine has dissolved (do not boil), 2-3 minutes. Stir into the strawberry mixture.
5. Divide mixture among 4 serving glasses. Chill until firm, 3-4 hours.
6. To serve, hull and dice the remaining ½ lb of strawberries. Spoon on top of the chilled jellied strawberries with a spoonful of whipped cream.

More Vibrant Fruit Dessert Ideas

Frozen Fruits Treats

Ideal on hot weather days, you can munch on these healthy frozen fruit pieces when you want to cool off. Line a rimmed baking sheet with parchment paper. In a single layer on the paper, arrange washed and patted dry fruit pieces such as sliced peaches or nectarines, raspberries, strawberries, blueberries, seedless grapes, banana, etc. Freeze; then, transfer to small freezer bags, label and date. Store in the freezer for up to a month. These frozen fruit pieces can also be used in smoothies and coulis (fruit sauce).

Fruit Coulis

This smooth fruit purée makes a great sauce over ice cream, meringue, cake, or other fruits. Easy and quick to prepare, it will become a part of your go-to dessert recipes. Keep refrigerated and use within a week.

1. Choose ripe fruits like berries (blueberries, raspberries, strawberries, blackberries), or grapes, about 4 cups. (If you choose fruit that will oxidize, like peaches and nectarines, you will need to add a bit of lemon juice to the purée to prevent browning.) Wash and pat them dry. Remove the stems and leaves, if present.
2. **Optional step:** In a large mixing bowl, combine the fruits with a few tablespoons of lemon juice, ¼ cup coconut sugar or a sweetener of your choice, 1 tbsp of Framboise liqueur or orange liqueur or 1 tsp of an essence of your choice like vanilla, rose water or orange blossom water. Cover and let macerate in the refrigerator for several hours or overnight.
3. In a blender, purée the fruit mixture to a smooth consistency, stop the blender before the mixture becomes foamy.

4. Pour the mixture in a sieve resting over a bowl. With a flexible spatula, press the mixture against the inner bottom of the sieve to catch as much of the pulp and seeds as possible, while filtering the sauce through. Discard the pulp and seeds. Taste the fruit sauce and add more sweetener if needed. If the consistency is too thick, add a little water. Your coulis is ready to be used.
5. If you can't find fresh, ripe fruits that you like, you can use frozen fruits that have been thawed and drained. Add some sweetener and purée in the blender.

2 – Wholesome and Nourishing Baking

Breads, Crackers, Muffins, and a Cake

"Paleotizing" my favorite baked recipes has required researching for non-offensive ingredients and creative tweaking. I know that it is possible to create food that is delicious and exciting.
I am the first to admit that nothing bakes as well and tastes as good as wheat flour!
However, I feel so much better after eating my "new and improved" occasional treats made with healthier and more wholesome ingredients.
And I certainly don't miss the *addictive* aspect and side effects of wheat-based baked goods.
The following recipes don't depend on exact measuring and skilled hands to be delicious and successfully achieved, but rather on fresh ingredients and a relaxed approach.
So, relax and have fun experimenting on your own.
You can't muff it up!

Quick and Simple Breads

Makes 8
Prep Time: 15 min.
Cooking Time: 15 min.

These little breads can be used as the bottom part of an open-faced sandwich, or enjoyed with a soup or stew. By using various herbs and spices, you can create a different batch each time.

A- 1 cup almond flour
¾ cup ground flaxseeds
2-3 tbsp hemp seeds
4 tsp baking powder
Pinch of Celtic salt

1 tbsp dried parsley
2 tbsp grated parmesan

B- 4 tbsp cold unsalted butter, cut into small cubes
4 egg whites

1. Preheat the oven to 350°F. Line a baking sheet with a piece of parchment paper.
2. In a large bowl, combine the **A** ingredients. With a fork, incorporate the butter until well combined.
3. In a separate bowl, with an electric beater on high speed, beat the egg whites until soft peaks form. Gently fold the egg whites into the dry ingredients until well combined.
4. Spoon the dough into 8 rounds on the baking sheet. With a spatula or your fingers, flatten the rounds to approximately ¾-inch thickness. Bake for about 15 minutes, or until golden brown. Allow to cool on a cooling rack for a few minutes.

Makes 1 loaf
Prep Time: 15 min.
Baking Time: about 25 min.

This is a wonderful moist bread that I flavour with fresh herbs from the garden.
Sometimes, I turn it into an **Olives and Sun-dried Tomato Bread** by adding 3 chopped green olives,
3 chopped sun-dried tomatoes, and ground hot pepper flakes for extra flavours. Other times, I add
curry powder and onion flakes. Feel free to add the savory essences that appeal to you.

A- Dry Ingredients:

¼ cup ground flaxseeds   1 tsp fine Celtic salt
2¼ cups almond meal   1 tsp baking soda

B- Wet Ingredients:

4 large eggs, lightly beaten   3 tsp coconut oil, melted
3 tsp honey or maple syrup   1 tbsp apple cider vinegar

C- 2 tsp each of fresh chives, basil, parsley and rosemary needles, finely chopped

1. Preheat the oven to 350°F. Prepare a loaf pan by buttering its sides and bottom.
2. In a large mixing bowl, combine the dry ingredients (**A**) and mix very well with a whisk.
3. In a medium bowl, mix the wet ingredients (**B**). Add the wet ingredients and the herbs to the dry ingredients. Mix well into a thick but smooth dough.
4. Pour the dough in the loaf pan; the dough will come about halfway up the sides.
5. Bake for about 25 minutes, depending on your oven, until a toothpick inserted in the middle comes out clean. Let cool in the pan before serving. Wrap with foil or food wrap. The bread should keep 3-5 days, if it doesn't get devoured before!

Serving Options:

1. **Spiced Tomato Butter**: To 1 cup of room-temperature **unsalted butter,** add 2 tbsp finely chopped **sun-dried tomatoes**, 2 tbsp finely chopped **chives**, ½ tsp grated **garlic**, ½ tsp **harissa** or hot pepper sauce, and a pinch of ground **cumin**. Combine well into a creamy consistency. Use on warm bread slices, on steamed vegetables, and baked potatoes.
2. **Prune and Blue Cheese Butter**: In a food processor, combine ½ cup of room-temperature **unsalted butter**, 3-4 **pitted prunes**, and ¼ cup room-temperature **blue cheese** of your choice. Pulse until a smooth consistency is achieved. Use on warm bread slices and crackers.
3. **Velvety Chicken Spread**:
   a. In a medium size pan, bring 2-3 cups **chicken broth** to a simmer. Add 1 skinless, boneless **chicken breast**, 1 tbsp **onion flakes**, a pinch of **salt and pepper**, and ½ tsp **curry powder**. Poach the chicken, uncovered, until the juices run clear when you make an incision in the middle, about 8-10 minutes. Let cool for a few minutes in the poaching broth. Cut in chunks. Reserve the poaching liquid to add to the next step, and to flavour a soup or to steam some rice.
   b. In a food processor, process the chicken chunks with a few tablespoons of the poaching liquid. Add ¼ cup **mayonnaise**, and ¼ cup **mango chutney**. Process until well combined and smooth. Taste and adjust the seasoning if necessary. Transfer to a serving dish, garnish with chopped coriander, and serve at room temperature or chilled. Cover and refrigerate the unused portion. This spread is great on the bread slices, on crackers (see recipe below) and as a dip with vegetable sticks.

To slowly break the sugar addiction, when you are craving sugar, drink water and eat more vegetables.
You will notice that within days, the cravings are much less fierce and frequent.

Makes about 36 (depending on size)
Prep Time: 30 min.
Baking Time: approx. 25-30 min.

Delicious with any spread, these crackers are surprisingly satisfying.
Stored in a closed container, they remain fresh for 4-5 days. Even though the dry ingredient list contains buckwheat, these crackers are wheat and grain free. Buckwheat, a grain-like seed, is related to sorrel, knotweed and rhubarb. Because it is its seeds that are eaten, it is considered a pseudo-cereal.
Note: To flatten the crackers, you will need a rolling pin.

A- Dry Ingredients:

½ cup ground almonds	1 tbsp hemp seeds
½ cup ground flaxseeds	1 tsp ground hot pepper
¼ cup buckwheat flour	1 tbsp coconut sugar
¼ cup toasted ground sesame seeds	1 tbsp onion flakes
2 tbsp coconut flour	1 tsp black pepper
2 tbsp psyllium husks	1 tsp salt

B- Wet Ingredients:

¾ cup cold water
3 tbsp extra-virgin olive oil

To finish: ⅓ cup olive oil, 1 tbsp toasted sesame seeds

1. Preheat the oven to 325°F. Line 2 cookie sheets with a piece of parchment paper.
2. In a medium bowl, combine all dry ingredients and stir. Add cold water and olive oil. Stir until the dough forms a ball. With a knife, divide the ball into 2 portions and set aside.
3. Sprinkle some buckwheat flour on your counter or table. Sprinkle your rolling pin with some flour. Roll one portion of the dough, from the centre to the outer edges, into ⅛" thickness. To even the edges, use a knife or a pizza cutter.
4. To transfer the flattened cracker dough to the parchment-covered cookie sheet, wrap it around the rolling pin; then, unravel it over the parchment paper. Brush with some olive oil and sprinkle with toasted sesame seeds. With a knife or a pizza cutter, cut the dough into 2" square crackers, or any shape or size you like.
5. Set the cookie sheet aside and repeat Steps 3-4 with the remaining portion of dough.
6. Bake for about 20 minutes. Remove any outside crackers that are already crispy. Continue baking for another 5-10 minutes or until the crackers are light brown and crispy. Keep an eye on them so they don't burn.

Makes 12
Prep Time : 25 min.
Cooking Time : 20-23 min.

These vegetable muffins, full of nutrients, are "fiber-licious",
even for the individual not convinced that wheat-free baked goods can be more than palatable.

A- Wet Ingredients

1 cup of finely grated carrots
1 cup finely grated zucchini
4 eggs, lightly beaten

1 tsp vanilla
2 tbsp maple syrup
⅓ cup water

B- Dry Ingredients

2 cups ground almonds
¼ cup ground flaxseeds
¼ cup hemp seeds
2 tbsp chia seeds
½ tsp baking soda
1 tsp baking powder

½ tsp salt
1 tbsp orange zest
½ tsp each ground cinnamon and nutmeg
½ cup raisins
½ cup chopped nuts of your choice
(pine nuts, cashews, walnuts)

C- ¼ cup melted coconut oil

1. Preheat the oven to 350ºF. Line a muffin tin with 12 muffin paper cups, or lightly grease the tin with some melted coconut oil.
2. In a large bowl, whisk all the wet **A** ingredients.
3. In a medium bowl, whisk the dry **B** ingredients together.
4. Pour the melted oil in the wet ingredients mixture and whisk together.
5. Pour half the dry ingredients into the wet mixture; mix with a wooden spoon. Add the rest of the dry ingredients and mix until combined.
6. Fill each muffin hole ¾ of the way to the top, leaving room for expansion. If you like, you can garnish each muffin with a thin slice of zucchini.
7. Bake for 20-23 minutes, or until a toothpick inserted in the centre of a muffin comes out clean. Cool for a few minutes before transferring each muffin to a cooling rack.

Home is not necessarily where I live.
I am at home where I can 'park' my belongings, and feel understood and loved.

Serves 8-10
Prep Time for the
icing: 24 hours
Prep Time for the cake: 20 min.
Baking Time: 35 min.

This delicious gluten-free cake is so moist that everyone will be amazed it is made without wheat flour. Most wheat-free cakes seem to sink in the middle when they are cooling. No worries; it doesn't affect the taste. You can cover the top with icing or vanilla-flavoured whipped cream, and garnish with fresh berries. In an airtight container, it will keep at room temperature for a few days.

Icing:

2 tubs of 500 g each of plain Greek yogurt
(I like the *Oikos* brand)
1 tsp orange zest
1-2 tbsp maple syrup

Pinch of cinnamon
Fresh fruit to garnish
Optional glaze: 2-3 tbsp orange marmalade

Cake:

1-2 tbsp soft butter
6 eggs, separated
½ cup coconut sugar
1 tbsp orange zest
1 tsp vanilla extract

½ tsp ground cinnamon
2 cups ground almonds
A pinch of Celtic salt
4-5 tbsp orange juice

1. **Icing:** For the icing, place the yogurt in a large sieve lined with a double layer of cheese cloth. Gather the corners to close and tie with a piece of string. Set the sieve over a large bowl to collect the liquid, and refrigerate for at least 24 hours or until the strained yogurt is firm.
2. **Cake:** Preheat the oven to 350°F.
3. With soft butter, grease the sides and bottom of a 9-inch spring-form pan. Line the bottom with a lightly greased piece of parchment paper. Set aside.
4. In a large bowl, beat with a hand mixer the egg yolks, sugar, orange zest, vanilla and cinnamon for about 5 minutes until the mixture thickens and turns a lighter colour.
5. Gently mix in the almonds, the salt and the orange juice.
6. In a medium bowl, beat the egg whites until stiff peaks form. Gently fold ⅓ of the egg whites into the egg yolk-almond mixture until combined. Gently fold in the rest of the egg whites until combined.
7. Pour the mixture in the prepared spring-form pan. Bake in the preheated oven for about 30 minutes, until the cake pulls away from the sides of the pan, and the top is golden and firm to the touch.
8. Run a knife between the edge of the cake and the pan. Let the cake cool in the pan on a rack for about 10 minutes. Unmould and let cool completely on the rack before icing or decorating.
9. **Icing :** In a medium bowl, whisk together the strained yogurt, the orange zest, the maple syrup and the cinnamon until well combined. Using a palette knife or a spatula, spread the icing over the cooled cake. Garnish with fresh fruits. If desired, melt the marmalade in a small saucepan and brush over the fruits.

3 – Sinful but Healthful Treats

Truffles and Fudge

Easy desserts that will please the young and the chronologically challenged.

Bonus: They all have a high-fiber content!

Sensual Jewel-like Truffles

Makes 16-20 truffles
Prep Time: 15-20 min.

Addictive!
Your guests and especially the children will
love these little balls of goodness!
Easy and quick to prepare, it is your food
processor that does all the hard work.
Use whatever dried fruit you already have or can find.

½ cup each dried cranberries and dried apricots
¼ cup each candied ginger and dried cherries
½ cup raisins
⅓ cup unsweetened shredded coconut
2 tbsp liquid honey or maple syrup
Zest of an orange

2 tbsp orange juice
¼ -½ tsp vanilla
To garnish: ½ cup ground almond

1. In a food processor, chop together all dried fruits and coconut until just combined. Add honey, orange zest, juice, and vanilla. Pulse until mixture clumps together and the fruits are chopped in very fine pieces.
2. Gather about 1 tsp of the mixture in your hands, and roll in a ball or shape in a cube. Roll in ground almond to coat all surfaces. Store in an airtight container in the refrigerator. It can keep for 1 week. Maybe! Serve with hot tea.

Nutty Carrot Truffles

Makes about 45 small truffles
Prep Time: 20 min.

Not too sweet, not too big, these healthy orange truffles are perfect after dinner with a nice cup of herbal tea.
You can adjust the quantity and the variety of spices to your liking.

3 medium carrots, peeled and chopped
¾ cup raw walnuts or almonds
½ cup raw cashews
½ cup soft Medjool dates, pitted and chopped
2 tsp finely grated orange zest

1 tsp ground cinnamon
½ tsp ground ginger
¼ tsp ground nutmeg
⅛ tsp ground clove
Pinch of salt

1. In a food processor, process the carrots until finely ground.
2. Add the rest of the ingredients and process until the nuts and the dates are chopped very finely and well incorporated into the carrots. (When pinched between your fingers, the mixture should be moist enough to hold together. If not, add 1 or 2 more pitted dates.)

3. Using your hands, roll the mixture into small balls. Refrigerated in an airtight container, the truffles will keep for up to 4 days.

Nutty Lemon Truffles

Makes about 45 small truffles
Prep Time: 20 min.

These delicious little bites are great as a snack or as a light dessert with a cup of tea, iced or hot. They are pictured here with the **Nutty Carrot Truffles**.

1 cup of raw cashews or almonds
1 cup of unsweetened desiccated coconut
Zest of 2 large lemons
1 soft Medjool date, pitted
1 tsp vanilla
1 tsp lemon juice
1 tsp cold water
2 tbsp maple syrup
A pinch of salt

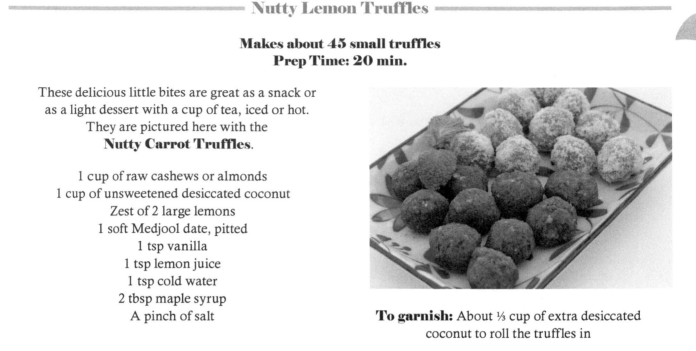

To garnish: About ⅓ cup of extra desiccated coconut to roll the truffles in

1. In a food processor, place all the ingredients, except the coconut for the garnish. Pulse just until the nuts and the coconut are ground, and the mixture is smooth.
2. Using your hands, roll the mixture into small balls. Roll the balls in the extra coconut to coat. Refrigerate in an airtight container until firm. They will keep for up to 4 days.

Spanish No-bake Chocolate Fudge

Makes 12-16 pieces
Prep Time: 5 min.
Melting Time: 5 min.
Chilling Time: 30 min.

An all-natural ingredient fudge with a silky-smooth texture to be savored slowly by letting it melt in your mouth.
Sure to make any chocolate lover very happy.
Ready in 45 minutes!
Can you wait?

½ cup of coconut oil
½ cup cocoa powder
½ cup almond butter
¼ cup maple syrup

½ tsp Celtic salt
1 tsp vanilla
Optional: Pinch of ground cinnamon
and hot red pepper

1. In a small saucepan, melt the coconut oil over low heat.
2. In a food processor, add all the ingredients with the melted oil. Process until well blended and smooth.
3. Line a plastic container with a piece of wax paper larger than the container; spread the chocolate mixture over the wax paper, smoothing the surface.
4. Refrigerate until firm, about 30 minutes. To serve, use the wax paper to lift the slab out of the container and place on a cutting board. Cut into small pieces. Refrigerate until serving time.

Extra Nourishment

These herbal and spicy mixes are great toppings for various dishes;
they are easy to blend and are full of low-calorie flavours.

Cheese-like Nutritional Yeast Sprinkle

Different than the active dry yeast or brewer's yeast, nutritional yeast is a dried and deactivated form of the microorganism *Saccharomyces cerevisiae*. Rich in energizing vitamin B and vitamin B_{12}, it is a nutrient essential for nerve functioning mainly found in animal foods. A generous sprinkling of nutritional yeast adds a nutty and cheese-like flavour to soup, steamed vegetables and baked savory dishes. It can keep refrigerated in a jar or in the freezer for 1 year or more. This low-sodium sprinkle can be added on salads, baked potatoes, etc. You can add other dried herbs like oregano and basil, and spices like fennel seeds and cumin seeds.

Combine the following ingredients in a 1-cup glass jar; label and date.

¼ cup nutritional yeast
¼ cup dried onion flakes
2 tbsp toasted sesame seeds
2 tbsp dried parsley

½ tsp dried garlic
¼ tsp Celtic salt
A pinch of black pepper

Parmesan Substitute

Easy to make, you can sprinkle it on anything you like. In a food processor, put equal amounts of **raw almonds** (or other nuts like walnuts or pine nuts) and **nutritional yeast**. Pulse until the texture looks like parmesan cheese. Store in a glass jar in the refrigerator. Label and date.

Gluten-free Option for Baking Powder

To help your wheat-free baked goods to rise, baking powder is often recommended in the ingredient list. It is best to use a gluten-free and aluminum-free product, if you can find one. If you cannot find one, it is easy to make your own by combining in a screw-top glass jar **2 parts of cream of tartar** and **1 part baking soda**. Shake to combine. Label and date. Replace after 1 year.

No-Salt Seasoning Mix

Find your favorite dry herbs, spices and other seasoning and create your own mix to sprinkle on food where salt is needed. Here is a suggestion: Mix together the following ingredients and store in a glass jar. Label and date.

1 tbsp dried parsley
1 tsp dried thyme
1½ tsp dried basil
1 tsp dried oregano
1 tbsp dehydrated onion flakes

½ tsp hot red pepper or chili powder
¼ tsp garlic powder
½ tsp celery seeds
½ tsp dried dill

Flavoured Salts

These simple salt blends will enhance the flavours of your salads and grilled foods.
Just a pinch, as a finishing touch on top of your dish, is necessary.
Stored in closed containers, these blends will keep up to 6 months.

A. Mint and Citrus: in a spice grinder, grind 1 tsp **citrus zest** (either lime, lemon, orange, grapefruit, or a combination) with 1 tsp dried **mint leaves**. Add this mixture to ¼ cup of **Fleur de sel**. Pour in a glass container and label. <u>Optional</u>: add 2 tsp freshly chopped chives.

B. <u>Herbal Lemon</u>: To ¼ cup **Fleur de sel**, add 1 tsp **lemon zest**, 1 tsp fresh **thyme** finely chopped, and 1 tsp fresh **rosemary** finely chopped. You can also add fresh **chives** and **parsley**, finely chopped. Pour in a glass container and label.

C. <u>Sweet and Exotic</u>: In a glass container, combine ¼ cup **Fleur de sel**, 1 tsp toasted **sesame seeds**, ½ tsp **curry powder** and ½ tsp **maple sugar**. Shake to mix well, and label.

Mediterranean Herb & Spice Mix

Mix together and store in a spice jar: 4 parts **basil**, 2 parts each **parsley**, **chervil**, **tarragon**, **rosemary**, 1 part **chives** and dried chopped **garlic**, dried **onion flakes** and **hot pepper flakes**.

Japanese Herb & Spice Mixes

If you enjoy Japanese food, you will love the following 3 spice blends. Used as finishing seasoning in place of salt, they add complex spicy flavours to soups, vegetables and rice noodle dishes. Store the mixes in glass jars, label and date.

1. Gomashio

This Japanese seasoning is great on almost everything, especially Asian dishes. You can purchase it at the store; however, creating your own allows you to control the freshness of the ingredients and the overall flavours of this seasoning. Feel free to adjust the quantities to your liking. In a spice grinder, grind all ingredients until well combined: ½ cup **sesame seeds**, white or black or a combination, 1 tbsp or less **Celtic salt,** 2 tbsp of any **dried seaweed** (kelp, nori, etc.)

2. Nourishing Japanese Sprinkle Mix

This delicious blend is great sprinkled on omelets, soups, salads, and anything else you can think of.

A. In a spice grinder, grind together ¼ cup **toasted almonds** or **pine nuts** with ¼ cup **dried goji berries**, 2 tbsp **flaxseeds**, and 1 sheet of chopped **nori (dried seaweed)** until well ground and blended.

B. Transfer to a screw-top glass jar. Add 2 tbsp **chia seeds**, 2 tbsp **hemp seeds**, 1 tsp (or less) **ground hot red pepper**, 1 tsp each of **white sesame seeds** and **black sesame seeds**. Close the lid and shake to mix well. Label, date and refrigerate. It will keep for 1-2 weeks.

3. Exotic Shichimi Togarashi

This popular blend is used to flavour fish dishes, soups, and grilled meats. Its spiciness combined with its subtle citrus and sea notes make this blend tasty and unique. You can find it in some Asian grocery stores or make it yourself with this easy recipe.

A. In a spice grinder, grind together ½ sheet of **nori (dried seaweed)**, 1 tbsp **dried mandarin peel**, 1 tbsp ground **cayenne pepper**, 3 tsp **white sesame seeds**, 1 tsp **poppy seeds**, 1 tsp ground **ginger**, ¼ tsp ground **Szechuan pepper**, 1 tsp **hemp seeds**.

B. Transfer to a screw-top glass jar. Close the lid and shake to mix well. Label, date and refrigerate. It will keep up to 2 months.

Food that has been prepared lovingly and mindfully,
not only excites the taste buds,
but on its way down to the stomach,
<u>touches</u> the heart and becomes coated with loving gratitude for the chef.

Gratitude

To create something, you must first have a dream.

I couldn't have created this nourishment book without the support, the encouragement, and the spiritual and emotional *nourishment* from the people who held the space for me and this project. The loving support and assistance I received from you made me feel like I was carried on a magical carpet to complete this journey; and because of your supporting presence and encouraging words, I could not NOT have reached my destination! I owe all of you my most heart-felt gratitude.

Always surround yourself with people who motivate and inspire you.

Philip, *l'amour de ma vie*, my precious husband and life partner, for always being next to me for yet another BIG project! I wouldn't be able to successfully accomplish as much with most of my sanity intact without your unwavering assistance, your steady fire energy and your loving patience. Besides being my hero, you are one of the most treasured gifts in my life.

Robert G Allen, my coach and mentor, for challenging me into writing this book.
Thank you for sharing your wisdom and expertise so that I can become more of who I am meant to be.

To the creative Balboa Press team, for your assistance in making this project a reality.

To my clients, for the pleasure and the privilege of working with you, for teaching me as much as I share with you.

And you, my readers, who are looking for answers to regain and maintain vibrant health; even though I haven't met you yet, I wish you the very best, especially a long, happy and vibrant life. May you find this nourishment-for-wellness book useful, practical and life-transforming for you and your loved ones. Thank you for investing in this book and sharing it with others. I welcome your comments, questions and feedback on my website at www.olivestolychees.com.

And finally, my deepest gratitude goes to my Divine Connections
for their daily loving guidance, creative inspiration, and protection.

From the bottom of my heart,
Merci! Merci! Merci!
I LOVE you all!
Namasté!

This book is **Volume 2** of the *Olives to Lychees* Collection focusing on nourishment for wellness.
If you would like to experiment with more Everyday Mediter-asian Paleo spa recipes and learn about the Art and the Pleasure of Eating Well, what makes us ill and gain weight, and the best foods to eat, make sure you get your copy of **Volume 1** *Olives to Lychees, Everyday Mediter-asian Spa Cuisine*, a nourishment-for-wellness book to resolve health and weight issues.

Thank you for allowing me to be part of your life.

Merci beaucoup et bon appétit!

*May you be blessed with an abundance of vibrant health, wealth, success and happiness
above and beyond what you could ask or imagine.
You deserve it, and so does your loved ones!*

Your friend, your witness, your cheerleader
Marie-Claire

Remember:
*No need to fuss to nourish and flourish.
Choose real fresh foods.
Cook from your heart.
Enjoy with family and friends.*

Resources and Recommended Reading

Books

1. *Smart Moves: Why Learning Is Not All in Your Head*, by Carla Hannaford (Great Ocean Publishers, 1995)
2. *Essential Oils Desk Reference Fifth Edition,* Compiled by Life Science Publishing, 2011
3. *Free Your Creative Spirit,* by Vivianne & Christopher Crowley (Walking Stick Press, 2001)
4. *Health Building, the Conscious Art of Living Well, A Complete Health Program for People of All Ages. Designed by the Internationally Renowned Doctor Who Developed Polarity Therapy*, by Dr. Randolph Stone, D.O., D.C. (CRCS Wellness Books, 1985)
5. *Polarity Therapy Certification Training Manual 2*, by Sher Smith (published by Realizing Your Potential, 2006)
6. *Home Spa Detox,* by Josephine Collins (Ryland Peters & Small, 2005)
7. *Inner Beauty, Discover Natural Beauty and Well-being with the Traditions of Ayurveda,* by Reenita Malhotra Hora (Chronicle Books, 2005)
8. *Instructions of Anatomical Charts of Internationally Standardized Acupoints,* Compiler-in-Chief Yan Zhenguo (Shanghai University of T.C.M Press)
9. *Lit From Within, A Simple Guide to the Art of Inner Beauty,* by Victoria Moran (Harper San Francisco, 2004)
10. *Pleasure Healing, Mindful Practices & Sacred Spa Rituals for Self-Nurturing,* by Mary Beth Janssen (New Harbinger Publications Inc., 2009)
11. *Quinta Essentia,* by Morag Campbell (Masterworks, 1995)
12. *Radiant Body, Restful Mind, A Woman's Book of Comfort,* by Shubhra Krishan (New World Library, 2004)
13. *Spa Magic, Creating a spa at home – with healing, rejuvenating, and beautifying recipes from spas around the world,* by Mary Muryn (Perigee, 2002)
14. *The Acupressure Atlas,* by Bernard C. Kolster, M.D. and Astrid Waskowiak, M.D. (Healing Arts Press, 2007)
15. *The Artist Inside, A Spiritual Guide to Cultivating Your Creative Self,* by Tom Crockett (Broadway Books, 2000)
16. *The Complete Guide to Reducing Stress*, by Chrissie Wildwood, (Piatkus, 1998)
17. *The Polarity Process, Energy as a Healing Art*, by Franklyn Sills (North Atlantic Books, 2002)
18. *Yoga for a New You, Relaxed, Energetic, Young, Confident,* (DK New York, 2012)

Magazines

Paleo Magazine
Simply Gluten Free

Index

The **bolded text** represents the recipe titles.

Lightning Source UK Ltd.
Milton Keynes UK
UKOW07f1613150917

309190UK00003B/10/P